March 17, 2009

Plus Sign on the Roof

+

To my good friend and mentor Professor Ted Gatchel,

Happy St. Patrick's Day,

Semper Fidelis

Chris

Plus Sign
on the Roof

Paul Van K. Thomson

ST. BEDE'S PUBLICATIONS
PETERSHAM, MASSACHUSETTS

Printed in the United States of America

96 95 94 93 92 91 90   5 4 3 2 1

Library of Congress Cataloging-in-Publication Data

Thomson, Paul van K (Paul van Kuykendall), 1916–
Plus sign on the roof/Paul van K. Thomson
p. cm.
ISBN 0-932506-86-0
1. Thomson, Paul Van K. (Paul van Kuykendall), 1916–
2. Converts, Catholic—United States—Biography.
3. Catholic Church—United States—Clergy—Biography.
4. Anglican use churches—United States—Clergy—Biography.
5. Episcopal Church—Clergy—Biography.
6. Anglican Communion—United States—Clergy—Biography. I. Title.
BX4668.T53A3   1990
282'.092—dc20   90-46842
(B)   CIP

Contents

Foreword

I am a Roman Catholic priest. I teach in a Roman Catholic college and assist the pastor of a Roman Catholic parish, where I say Mass regularly. I also have a wife, to whom I have been married for over forty years. We have seven adult offspring, all of whom have their own homes and careers. And we have twelve grandchildren at this writing.

Whenever I am asked—and I have been asked often—how this most unusual situation could have been possible, I do generally take the time to explain that I was ordained in 1983 under a Pastoral Provision extended by the present Pope to married former Episcopal priests who have become Catholics. This was something my wife and I did in 1949, without any thought that I would ever be permitted to be ordained as a Catholic priest. We just wanted to live as Catholics because we had become convinced that, as Vatican II was later to say, "For it is through Christ's Catholic Church alone, which is the universal help towards salvation, that the fullness of the means of salvation can be obtained" (*Unitatis Redintegratio*).

Even if time actually permits me to say all that, I always have to end up saying, "But it is really quite a long story." This book is that long story. It is a very personal book about a lifelong spiritual journey and it is dedicated to all who have been my companions along the way.

Plus Sign on the Roof

✚

ONE

From a Window
in Weehawken

Probably the first real look I had of the world was through a
window that looked out on a street in Weehawken, New
Jersey, a rather dreary town on the palisades of the Hudson
where I was born on the fourteenth of December in 1916. At
that moment the European center of civilization was in the
process of committing suicide in the course of what was
coming to be referred to as The Great War. The *New York
Times* described it in various ways as a battle for freedom
against the German tyranny that had ravaged poor little
Belgium. In Weehawken, however, there were a large
number of German-Americans—to say nothing of Irish in
New York—who disagreed. In any case, what was really
going on was no more apparent to most people than it was
to me.

Not much of historical importance had ever happened in
Weehawken since the day when Alexander Hamilton was
killed there in a duel with Aaron Burr. This unhappy incident was the subject of a very modest memorial bust of
Hamilton mounted on a rock that adorned a little park on
the palisades above the reputed site of the duel. Burr had no

3

memorial. Weehawken was a Republican island in the vast sea of Democrats which was called Hudson County and had its political center in Jersey City, where the conventional rhetoric was Jeffersonian.

A more stimulating sight than that of the bust of Hamilton was the steady flow of Hudson River traffic beneath the skyline of New York. Against that dramatic background, which was then dominated by the sixty soaring stories of the Woolworth Building, I recall seeing the wonder of the German reparation zeppelin, once called by the Germans the *ZR–3*, but re-christened as the *Los Angeles* when I saw it as a wondrous silver monster floating above the Hudson in1924.

I think my earliest memory is, however, of something having to do with the river that took place in 1919 on the docks of the town of Hoboken, which adjoined Weehawken and boasted of its Stevens Institute of Technology and some of the finest German beer served anywhere in America during the dry years of Prohibition. On the Hoboken docks I was taken to witness the return of some American troops who disembarked there from France as they returned from the Great War. I remember being excited by the cheering, the flags, the bands and the sight of some strange big barrels that were half-hidden in a corner under canvas. Here was, of course, a bit of the end of a chapter in the history of a conflict whose sequence would involve my whole generation.

My window in Weehawken thus opened on signs of the movement of very big changes in distant places that affected things even in our river town at the "other end" of the Forty-Second Street Ferry. And these changes were connected in my imagination with bands and flags and men coming home from war. It was almost inevitable that very early on in my life—when I was six or seven—I developed a passion for toy soldiers and war games. Consequently, I was very disappointed to learn that my father, who was a mild-mannered railway clerk in poor health, had not been in the legions of warriors who had supposedly won the Great War.

Indeed, when I learned from my mother that she had once wanted to marry one of the returned warriors who came home to found a world-famous advertising agency, but had not done so because her parents had thought him "too wild," I concluded that they must have had very poor judgment. This feeling was, I suppose, connected with the fact that there was never enough money in our family. Railway clerks were poorly paid, as were public school teachers in Union City, where my mother taught eighth grade English classes. My maternal grandmother lived with us in our apartment and doted on me, her only grandchild. There was, so far as I could tell, no great romantic passion in the lives of my parents, whose most intense expressions of emotion were aroused by bills they could barely afford to pay.

My father, poor man, rejoiced in the name of Walter Scott Thomson and, like his famous namesake, loved tales of the Middle Ages. But one evening as he was reading to me about the Crusades, when he came on the name of the poor French knight called Walter the Penniless, he sadly remarked that this should have been his name too.

His parents, John and Mary Thomson, had emigrated from Scotland, but this was a subject of which I heard very little, for my mother thought it more important for me to learn the history of her father's family. They were the Kuykendalls, who had come to the Hudson Valley from Holland in the seventeenth century. My mother saw a certain snob value in that name, which some claimed was really van Kuykendall. It was on the basis of this claim that I acquired a very difficult middle name and the curious initials "van K." I don't know that the name Kuykendall in itself implied a great distinction. A man I met once in Amsterdam informed me over a glass of Holland gin that it seemed to mean nothing more than "little chicken in the valley."

Not a great deal was ever said about my maternal grandmother's family, except that her parents had emigrated from Ireland where, it was rumored, she had two uncles who were Catholic priests. She had been born Katherine Daly, but if her parents had indeed been Catholics in Ireland, they had lost their faith after coming to America, for their daughter knew little of it and thought she had probably been brought up as some sort of Protestant, possibly Methodist, but it did not seem to matter much to her. She was a kind, friendly, fun-loving woman who, as far as I could tell, seldom went to any church and numbered Catholics as well as Protestants among her many friends. It mattered little to her what church they attended as long as they were loyal Democrats.

Religion was, however, very important to both my mother and father. It is my impression, looking back on my childhood, that religion was much more important to each of them individually than they ever were to each other. Both of them had become Episcopalians as young adults, something which for my mother at least represented a movement closer to Catholicism, to which she had been attracted from girlhood. Late in her life she confided in me that she had often thought in her youth and before her marriage not only of becoming a Catholic but also of becoming a nun. In any case, both of my parents attended the Episcopal church regularly, and my religious education was carefully nurtured by faithful attendance at Sunday School in the parish hall of Grace Episcopal Church in Union City, where I had been baptized as an infant.

My father was especially active in church affairs, was a member of the vestry, and frequently served as an usher on Sundays. One of the things I most remember about him is hearing him say, "I would rather be a doorkeeper in the house of the Lord than a prince in the tents of the ungodly."

He said it with a smile, but he meant it most deeply.

His religious background had been in the tradition of the Reverend Thomas Campbell, a Scots-Irish immigrant minister of the Presbyterian variety, whose son Alexander Campbell finally broke away to help found one more American denomination. This group, called The Disciples of Christ by their founders, were sometimes also known as Campbellites and were notable for their strong objections to hierarchical church organizations and anything that might suggest Catholicism. Thus my father's becoming an Episcopalian was a radical change. But what made it even more so was the fact that he preferred the so-called High Church ritual and was much attracted by the Episcopal church called The Church of St. Mary the Virgin, which was located off Broadway in New York. This place was more than High Church; it was described as being Anglo-Catholic. The clergymen there were unmarried and were addressed as Father. Moreover, they wore Catholic vestments, observed Catholic saints' days, heard confessions in a Catholic confessional box, and conducted elaborate services that were as much as possible made to resemble a Catholic High Mass.

I am not sure when it was that I discovered that there were Episcopalians who actually believed that way in church. But I recall that it was a wonderful discovery. I was a highly imaginative only child, nurtured on reading about medieval heroes such as Roland and Lancelot, and I was much given to "dressing up" and acting out little dramas I created for myself. Love for magnificent music and liturgy came to me very easily.

Moreover, during my primary school years my circle of friends consisted of boys who, like myself, actually enjoyed school and delighted in devising elaborate games played with toy soldiers or acting out historical episodes in costumes. Thus it was that even the most modest ecclesiastical ceremony, such as the processions of the boy choristers in which I participated in our rather plain little parish church, served to stir my imagination and to evoke a nostalgic sense of the mystery and grandeur of what I supposed people had once experienced during the Middle Ages when just about everyone was a Catholic.

Almost as soon as I was able to read simple history books or adventure stories set in the past, I had a vivid sense of living in a present that had been created by a generally more attractive past. Learning, for example, that some of my Dutch ancestors had fought at the Battle of Saratoga and had thus advanced the Revolution of the colonists, struck me with the notion that what they had done was still affecting me. But I was not at all sure that I was glad about it. I failed to see what was really gained by separating from the British Empire, with all its splendid Anglican pageantry and what was still at that time so much territory, all of which was colored pink on the globe in my bedroom.

I disliked intensely what I had read about the Puritans of New England who had claimed freedom of worship for themselves but refused to grant it to others. As far as their conduct in England itself was concerned, I understood that the Puritans not only disapproved of Christmas but also executed Charles I, whose pictures at least suggested to me that he was actually an altogether dashing and attractive sort of man, who probably enjoyed Christmas and other feasts very much indeed.

As a consequence of my dislike for the New England Puritans, I grew in my dislike for the peculiarly American holiday called Thanksgiving Day. This impressed me unfavorably as a time when everyone had to eat turkey. I much preferred roast beef. It was also a time when we school children were forced to dress up either as Indians or Pilgrims. Of the two roles, I much preferred that of an Indian but almost always ended up dressed as a Pilgrim and compelled to say something dull but supposedly pious about how God had preserved the colony through the terrible winter.

Most of all I associated the Pilgrims and their dinner with dreary, boring visiting relatives who ate too much, drank too much, and showed their annual gratitude to the Almighty by either quarreling or going to sleep in their after-dinner chairs. The depth of my dislike and the intensity of my feeling about my image of New England Puritanism may be seen in the fact that when I was taken as an adolescent to see Plymouth Rock, I actually spit on the relic itself. Was this not the place where anti-Anglican dissenters were said to have first set foot on the American continent? My sense of history at that stage made this vulgar piece of adolescent gaucherie somehow something symbolically transformed into a blow struck for the memory of the good King Charles I, to whom Anglo-Catholics referred as a martyr.

Of course, when I was growing up as a boy in Weehawken my immediate link with the past was someone much closer than poor old King Charles the Martyr. It was my maternal grandmother, especially after my father's death during the summer of my tenth year. After that it became necessary for my mother to teach some night school classes in addition to her regular daytime work. Consequently I was often alone with my grandmother. This was an arrangement which I greatly enjoyed since my grandmother indulged me, thought I could do no wrong and did not hesitate to say so quite frequently.

My mother, on the other hand, had to be the authority figure who insisted that I should practice my hated piano lessons and do my household "chores," such as taking out the trash, emptying the water from the "ice box" and helping to keep the apartment clean. But my grandmother helped me to escape into the past and did some of the "chores" herself so that I could have more time to do such things as working out the Battle of Waterloo with my toy soldiers on the floor of my bedroom. And she often added to the ranks of my troops with purchases from local toy dealers or, on rare occasions, from the armies of F.A.O. Schwartz in New York.

She was in many ways a living voice of history for me. For example, she talked of the Great Blizzard of 1888 so vividly that to this day I sometimes think I lived through it myself. Or she told, with a lot of laughter, of how as a young girl going courting she always wore a big hoop skirt if the young man was not to her fancy so that there would be no room for him to sit up in the seat of the buggy and he would have to lead the horse on foot. She never did tell what she did under circumstances in which the young man was to her liking. And I certainly never dared to ask her. I was aware, of course, that in the world in which she had grown up proper young ladies never showed their legs for the simple reason that they did not have legs. Such appendages were discreetly spoken of as limbs, and I can still recall my grandmother's description of what had happened to one of her girlhood friends as: "She broke one of her limbs." Which one it was, she never said.

Several times she took me to the annual Memorial Day parades when local war heroes marched through the streets of Weehawken in all their old uniforms—or parts thereof— and local politicians celebrated victories at war monuments while they praised the fallen with windy rhetoric. Among the most honored participants in these parades, upon whom I gazed with awe, were three or four almost corpse-like old fellows in blue uniforms who were respectfully transported in open so-called touring cars marked with signs reading Grand Army of the Republic. These ancient warriors were, I loved to imagine, survivors of the bloody hills at Gettysburg, of the line where Pickett's rebel charge had broken. More likely, of course, they survived because they were clerks in the Quartermaster Corps, who knew how to turn down requests for supplies by saying, "We don't have enough for ourselves." But I had not yet been to war and did not know of such things.

My grandmother, however, would look at the old men in blue and remember for me about how she had stood as a child on the steps of the post office in Catskill, New York, when the news came that Lincoln had been assassinated.

"There was a man standing there," she would say, "who was known as a rebel and a Copperhead. When he heard the news, he was heard to say Good! And that very night he was struck dead by a heart attack, which was really the hand of God."

In such ways, then, the past came alive for me through my grandmother's memories, but my romantic attachment to bygone times took on new proportions when in September, 1929 I entered Weehawken's Woodrow Wilson High School and began the study of first-year Latin, a subject which was then very wisely required of all students who aspired to go to college.

I became fascinated by the Romans and by their wonderful language. Thus I persevered in my Latin studies beyond that first required year until, together with two other devoted students, I had gone the full four years through Caesar's wars, Cicero's civic struggles and Vergil's tale of Aeneas. In fact, I became so taken with Vergil that I even tried to produce a poem of epic proportions in heroic hexameters which was to deal with the love of Caesar for Cleopatra. Happily this work never got very far and ended up as a few pages pasted in my mother's scrapbook of my literary productions. She did not read Latin and was spared all knowledge of how dreadful my poem was.

However dreadful my Latin poetry was, my love of Latin as a precise, beautiful language was nonetheless genuine. So was the attraction of the classical Roman world its study had disclosed to me. I venture to think that my very untypical response to that world and my pleasure in reading its language were, in the Providence of God, really signs of the direction my life would finally take. It would not be altogether surprising when I came to recognize Rome as the true center of the whole mainstream of Christianity, and responded profoundly to the Latin liturgy, for the way had been prepared for that when I first made the acquaintance of Caesar, Cicero, and Vergil. Indeed, to this day I find the pedestrian, plodding English of the contemporary Catholic liturgy sometimes a cause to shudder and regret the death of so much beauty that once adorned the worship of the Roman Mass everywhere in the world.

Looking back on my adolescence in the secondary school years I spent at Woodrow Wilson High School, it seems evident that I was truly being formed and directed to become not only a Catholic but a priest, albeit a married one.

Certainly religion was a major concern. Of course, I experienced the usual adolescent difficulties with the biblical accounts of human origins, as well as with Jonah's whale, the parting of the Red Sea and miracles generally. Like St. Augustine in his youth I found much of the kind of history recorded in the Old Testament distasteful, and I used to argue for hours with a Jewish girlfriend about what was to me the problem of why God should have chosen the Jews in the first place, for they seemed not to have been very faithful to Him. In fact, He appeared to be angry with them much of the time. And the prophets kept saying that it was with good reason.

But Fundamentalism about the Bible was not the outlook of the Episcopal Church and after reading Bishop Gore and other very enlightened Anglican divines, I quickly saw that the Bible ought not to be read as if it were a natural history book and without any sense of the development of cultures. I also read popular Protestant Modernist preachers like Harry Emerson Fosdick and was put off by the way they simply assumed that there had to be a rationalistic, empirical explanation for everything in religion, which was itself largely nothing more than a lofty scheme of ethics touched by noble emotions and clothed in meaningful myths.

My religion was basically what I took to be the historic Faith expressed in the Apostles Creed and attested to by the experience of millions. And it was a matter of faith—faith that could be shown to be reasonable. I felt then, as I have felt all my life, the tension between belief and skepticism and I have never known the absolute peace of total certitude, which makes for certain forms of fanaticism.

Visits to the services of various mainline Protestant churches with school friends convinced me that they were all very nice people searching for the Kingdom of God through scriptures, hymns, preaching, and what they called "fellowship." But it was not for me. What I was really hoping to discover was a church that laid claim to being the Kingdom of God searching for people, nice or not so nice. And in those days I certainly did not think I had found it when I accompanied Catholic friends to their Mass, where the Latin was, when audible, badly pronounced; the music was ghastly, and the religious art was utterly vulgar. As for the priest, he appeared bored by the whole performance, except when he delivered a brief sermon. Then he seemed mostly angry about something, but what he was angry about was none too clear.

With my continuing interest in religion there arose, as has often been the case, a problem about sex that was somewhat different from the problems on that subject generally being experienced by most of my male adolescent peers, most of whom talked about it constantly, pursued it when possible, and boasted of triumphs that were largely their own fantasies. I certainly shared in all that sort of thing and cared greatly for a number of the girls I met. But I was also wary of them. This was partly because I feared rejection more than I could say. Yet, there was another reason for my ambivalent attitude. As the time in school passed and we all had to start wondering what we were going to do with the rest of our lives, it seemed to me that I might very well decide to become an Episcopalian priest. But if I did that, it struck me that I should be unmarried always, like the Anglo-Catholics at the Church of St. Mary the Virgin. If I were to devote myself to the calling to serve Christ and humanity, it would have to be "all the way" and not something done professionally with time out for a private life or a family. I was not at all sure that I could handle that. I prayed a lot about this in front of a crucifix in my bedroom, but when I was with girls I seemed to keep giving evidence that the answer was for me to look around for some other calling.

So it came about that I spent time thinking that politics or possibly journalism would offer me more appropriate career choices. I had already developed quite an interest in politics during the 1928 Presidential campaign, which took place in my twelfth year—the year before I entered high school. I had always written bits of verse and pieces of prose, which no one thought much of but my mother. Some of my things were actually published on the children's page of the local paper, the *Hudson Dispatch*, which was largely a house organ for Frank Hague, the Democratic "boss" of Jersey City. During the course of my literary development, I had started writing letters to the editor of this somewhat grubby paper and was delighted when some of my views appeared in print. My youthful age was evidently not known to the person who permitted this to happen.

One of my letters to the editor was a fierce defense of Al Smith's right, as an American and a Catholic, to seek the Presidency of the United States. I launched a bombastic assault on the vicious anti-Catholic propaganda that marred the campaign of Smith's Republican opponents, who were promoting Herbert Hoover, who was to have the great misfortune to be elected on the very eve of the Great Depression.

After my letter appeared and it was disclosed that its author was a boy who had not quite reached his twelfth birthday, the local Democratic machine started having me speak at Smith rallies, as if I were a child evangelist, a boy wonder who had come like David to kill the Republican Goliath. All this had delighted me no end, and when I received a letter of thanks from the National Democratic Committee, I was, of course, convinced that someday I might run for President— but as an Episcopalian. There was, after all, a good deal of precedent for that.

Consequently, during all of my high school years I involved myself in campus politics and served as editor of the school weekly newspaper, member of the Student Council, and finally as President of that body, in which office I made a dreadful nuisance of myself by demanding that the school administration should give students more of a role in running the place.

My senior year in high school was the year 1932–33. We were in the Great Depression; unemployment was at 13 percent in the United States and was ravaging most of Europe, especially Germany and Britain. And things were not that good in Weehawken either. Roosevelt was getting himself elected President, but by that time I had decided that capitalism was dying and had gotten carried away by the fiery preacher's Socialist rhetoric of Norman Thomas at a big Socialist rally in the old Madison Square Garden. I decided to become a Christian Socialist, like some I had heard of in the Church of England. Moreover, I decided to combine radical politics of the so-called Social Gospel and my aspirations towards the clerical life and put to one side, for the time being, the question of clerical marriage.

As result of this very ill-considered decision, I presented myself to the rector of Grace Episcopal Church in Union CIty and informed him that I planned to go to Columbia University in the following fall to begin studies for the ministry. The Reverend George Porter Armstrong was somewhat astonished, for he had known me both as a chorister and as an altar boy and had seen nothing in my conduct to suggest that I was especially pious or touched in any special way by the Holy Spirit. But he was a kindly man and agreed to send me to talk to the bishop in Newark. Perhaps a successor of the Apostles would know how best to deal with such a case.

The Right Reverend Benjamin Martin Washburn, Bishop of the Episcopal Diocese of Newark, interviewed me and solemnly looked at my written request to become what is called a postulant for Holy Orders, the first of several steps leading to priestly ordination in the Episcopal Church. Bishop Washburn belonged to a now-vanished breed. He was all that used to be meant by the word gentleman, and he wore the dignity of his office with the plain style of the security of the Protestant Episcopal establishment, as it was then best represented by the Episcopal Divinity School in Cambridge, Massachusetts, surrounded by the fortifications of Harvard and the protective concern of the directors of several Boston Banks. As he talked with me, he explained that in the Episcopal Church there was what he called "a very real place" for those who preferred the High Church point of view. Of course, he never made clear just where this "real place" might be located. I suspect that he supposed that at Columbia, with its own Ivy League reasonableness, I would grow up and iron out my odd Anglo-Catholic wrinkles. In any event, he was then—as he always was thereafter—most kind to me when he informed me that he would accept me as one of his postulants for the Diocese of Newark.

Having obtained scholarship help from the venerable Society for the Promotion of Religion and Learning, I was subsequently admitted to Columbia in the freshman class which gathered there in the fall of 1933. The University authorities were duly informed that my plan was to study for the ministry. What they were not told was that I intended to change the world. I was then in my seventeenth year.

TWO

The Roaring Lions

Once upon a time there was a powerful football team at Columbia, whose totem symbol was a lion. This team won many games so that when its fans sang "Roar lion, roar," they really meant it and no one laughed. I know because I was there when such things happened. Moreover, I did a lot of roaring at Columbia, but I must confess that most of it had nothing to do with football.

I applied for admission to Columbia and did not apply elsewhere. Unlike Yale and Harvard, Columbia had no connection with Puritanism. Whatever it had become, its roots were impeccably Anglican. The place was, after all, founded in 1754 as King's College, under a royal charter from the most un-Puritanical George II. Since that time it had become one of the very few world-class universities in America and it was in New York, which I thought was certainly the greatest of all American cities.

When I was informed on May 12, 1933 that I would probably be in the Freshman class in the fall, I was greatly pleased and felt that George II could not have been quite so stupid as history said he was nor as uninspiring a figure as his portrait suggested. I even made a resolution to find out more about the life of the Reverend Samuel Johnson, who was the first President of King's College and a clergyman who, although he had been a Congregationalist and had graduated from Yale, had the great good sense to join the Church of England and enter the Anglican ministry, where he became the friend and correspondent of Bishop Berkeley. I did discover that he became an exponent of Berkeley's brand of idealism. After that, however, I never bothered to find out any more about him.

Quite on my own I decided to major in English literature as an appropriate undergraduate preparation for theological studies later on. I did so partly because it had been my best high school subject but also because I had the notion that it was concerned with human beings and their personal lives. At that time, of course, I had not yet met anyone who thought that poetry had no meaning or purpose other than its own existence. Nor had I encountered those who were to say that works of literature must be deconstructed by those highly skilled in linguistic analysis because the very notion of "meaning" in the common sense of that word is itself meaningless.

I chose to study creative works of literature because I thought what I later learned had been thought—somewhat before my time—by Aristotle, who wrote that poets are superior to writers of mere history because poets do not confine themselves to things that are supposed to have happened but write of what could happen, or what ought to happen, and present imitations of the actions of human beings at their best and at their worst. The poets, I thought, explored the souls of human beings and the hungers of the heart. They knew the value of clowns and the stature of heroes. They knew, as Vergil had known, "the tears at the heart of things." Men of religion had better know them, for the poets were the makers of the great myths; they were the ones who did awake what all people do asleep: they clothed experience with symbolic stories in order to interpret and cope with it. And some poets sometimes were disturbers of the peace and sources of trouble for those who tried to crush the discontented and those who wished to change the status quo.

Certainly, from the outset I was one who wanted to change the status quo of things as we found them at Columbia. I had plenty of company in my class, which—much to my astonishment—seemed to be made up of any number of former crusading Presidents of Student Councils and former editors of rebellious high school newspapers. I had thought I would be the only one. This was the first of many illusions about myself which I was forced to abandon at Columbia.

· The first target of critical attack had to do with the rather minor issue of the length of the dormitory cots, which were already under assault from older malcontents, such as Arnold Beichman, a sophomore who was a member of the august body known as The Student Board. The campus daily paper, the *Spectator*, reported that restless, tall members of the Socialist Club, the Student Board, and the feisty Freshman class found the dormitory cots to be both too short and too saggy. These rebels, of whom I was one, were reported to be planning to form what they called a "horizontal union" to strike against the cots. The more violent even planned a bed-burning demonstration in front of Low Library. In the end, of course, the college administrators prevailed by treating this issue with the generally effective benign neglect that so often marks the pattern of the best academic administrators. Nothing was done and we students quickly found other ways of disturbing the peace of the Dean and of filling the columns of the *Spectator*—known simply as "Spec"—with more serious sources of our constant discontent with the policies of our elders both on and off campus.

But before making any further contributions to the

sound and fury of our first days at Columbia, I decided that it would be appropriate for me—now a postulant for Holy Orders—to present myself at the office of the University Chaplain, who was in those days, like the President, at least nominally an Episcopalian. He thus constituted a somewhat vague link with the University's Anglican beginnings and an even vaguer link with God, about Whom the University took no official position, although its President had been known to invoke His name when commenting on current campus disturbances.

The Chaplain was, in any case, sufficiently vague to hold his post without offending anyone. Indeed at the time of his death some years later the *New York Times*, with customary insight, observed that next to religion Chaplain Raymond Knox's main interest was in rowing on the Hudson. The morning I kept the appointment I had made with him he greeted me in his office in Earl Hall wearing not the customary clerical attire but a rather stiff grey suit that was set off by a mildly blue tie surmounted by a starched Arrow collar. Being a smart-aleck Anglo-Catholic I addressed him as Father Knox, to which he replied with an appropriate cliche, saying, "Young man, I am a father, but I am not your father."

Not knowing quite how to respond to this clerical witticism, I proceeded to explain that I was a member of the freshman class and a postulant for Holy Orders from the Diocese of Newark. His reaction to this was rather like that of the Whig Bishop of London, who is said to have responded to John Wesley's urgent appeal for missionary bishops to be sent to the North American colonies by saying, "This enthusiasm of yours, Mr. Wesley, is a dreadful thing." He suggested that at some future date I might want to have tea with the members of the campus Episcopal Club, which met somewhat infrequently. He also informed me that there were non-sectarian services held each noonday in St. Paul's Chapel. The preacher for that day would be a well-known swami, who was described as being "quite keen on Hindu psychology."

This bizarre interview terminated rather quickly with the suggestion, properly vague of course, that I might just possibly want to take the Chaplain's course on the letters of St. Paul some time while I was at Columbia. With that stimulating challenge ringing in my ears, I left feeling somewhat uncertain as to whether or not Chaplain Knox and I belonged to the same church.

That was a question I was to ask myself about any number of Anglican clergymen in the years to come and the answers were generally that we probably had the Book of Common Prayer as something we shared as members of the diverse Anglican Communion, which somehow defied all the laws of logic. But in the case of Chaplain Knox, even that was not an answer. Yet I suppose that this was precisely what made him the perfect person to serve as the official representative of religion at Columbia. He was, in a word, totally nondescript.

Coming out of Earl Hall, I passed a door marked Catholic Chaplain and it struck me that if I ever felt the need to talk with a clergyman on campus, I would probably go through that door. After all, it was standard High Church ecclesiology to say that there were really three kinds of Catholics: Roman, Orthodox, and Anglican. It did not matter that neither Roman Catholics nor Eastern Orthodox believed this. High Anglicans did and that led me to think that when I needed one, I would find a priest and a friend in the office of the Catholic Chaplain.

And so I did. He was Father George Ford, a priest for all people and all seasons. He was ecumenical long before the word became fashionable and lost its meaning. He was a truly great human being, the measure of whose greatness was the fact that he earned the undying enmity of Cardinal Spellman, after that prelate became Archbishop of New York in 1939.

It was to Father Ford that I went with all the doubts and difficulties inherent in preparing for the ministry at Columbia in those turbulent years in a University dominated by the pragmatism of John Dewey, which bred an illiberal liberalism that pretended to tolerate everything in the realm of ideas but brooked no opposition to what it deemed to be its own "enlightened self-interest." There were many mornings, especially in my first year, when I felt I had no place to take my confusion and my not infrequent hangovers except to Father Ford's Mass in the Newman Center. Of course, I could not receive Holy Communion, but after Mass, Father Ford welcomed me—as he welcomed everyone with genuine hospitality. And during Mass I heard the beautiful, precise Latin as he pronounced it, as if it were a gentle rain in the spiritual desert, which the University sometimes seemed to be, interposed between me and the remote God that I simply could not talk to anymore with any sense that he was really calling me to serve him.

A major source of my confusion about this and many other matters was the then famous Columbia course called Introduction to Contemporary Civilization in the West, simply known to undergraduates as "C.C." All students were required to take this two-year excursion into cultural history and current economic and political issues. When we graduated in 1937, the class voted C.C. the dullest course in the college, along with President Nicholas Murray Butler, who was voted Bore Number One, with Herbert Hoover as runner-up for that title.

I certainly agreed that Butler was a crashing bore and a primary example of how a man could be like a mathematical point, which has position but not magnitude. But for me there was nothing boring about C.C., which I experienced as something truly traumatic, with its arrogant assumption that social utility was the standard of value judgments, especially as social utility was then perceived by those faculty members who spent a lot of time in Washington constructing Franklin Roosevelt's New Deal.

C.C. was the "party line" of Columbia University, quite as much as the Baltimore Catechism was the standard teaching in parochial schools or the philosophy of so-called Thomism in Catholic colleges of that era. Perhaps its position was really more akin to that of Dialectical Materialism in Soviet universities, although such a thing would have been denied by John Herman Randall or the other high priests of the dogmas of Dewey.

For them—and so for C.C.—the great modern world (which incidentally was about to produce World War II) really began with Galileo and the telescope. The ancient world expressed itself in myths and speculative philosophy, which Francis Bacon and other empiricists had shown to be utterly useless. Of course the Christian Middle Ages drew heavily upon both myths and Greek philosophy and created for itself a "band box universe" in which the sky was the cover over the earthly stage upon which was played out the Drama of Salvation, with heaven above and hell beneath. In the Renaissance man began to rediscover his own wonderful powers, but things really got going in the right direction in the seventeenth century. Then it was that with the work of Descartes and Newton humanity began to break out of the closed, mythological world of the past and take the broad open path of experimental science and empirical philosophy. Of course, in this scenario there was no serious consideration of the thought of the great mathematician and Christian mystic Pascal.

The C.C. party line described the eighteenth century with an enthusiasm which that century would have repudiated. The so-called Age of Reason—which was also the age of the violent Terror of the French Revolution and the age of the rise of the Gothic tale of horror—was brightly described by bright young instructors as the wonderful time when God and tyrants died. Then it was that myths and metaphysics disappeared and gave way to a truly critical and instrumental approach to practical problems and the true pursuit of life, liberty, property and the earthly Paradise, which was best represented by the new United States, a true and pure example of Enlightenment. Indeed the essence of Enlightenment political philosophy was expressed in the American Declaration of Independence, whose enlightened author was, however regretfully, one of the major slave owners in the former colony of Virginia.

While it was never explicitly stated, one was given the impression that ever since the time of Voltaire and Jefferson, educated people generally shared the opinion that we could know only what we could perceive by our senses and test by experience. There was no legitimate basis for claims that there was somehow or other a so-called "spiritual" reality. Pope was correct when he declared that the proper study of mankind is man himself and Jeremy Bentham was equally correct when he concluded that progress consisted chiefly in creating ever-greater degrees of health and comfortable living for people everywhere. Such progress was seen as inevitable if human beings would conduct themselves rationally and make appropriate use of the natural and social sciences.

Many members of the departments of economics, political science, and sociology, we were informed, were temporarily away from the University for the express purpose of creating progress in the form of the New Deal. Once in a great while one or another of them would pay a brief visit or even lecture to students. But most of that dreary chore was left to young instructors. Meanwhile Columbia was doing its part to advance the enlightened liberal democracy, which had had its birth in the great eighteenth century, grew to maturity in the mind of John S. Mill in the nineteenth century, and was now flourishing in the sunlight of the minds of Charles Beard, John Dewey, Stuart Chase, and Rexford G. Tugwell.

Moreover, the newer version of economic liberalism, as set forth by John Maynard Keynes, had now arrived at a point at which correct action by democratic governments could regulate and virtually eliminate the cyclic depressions of capitalism. It was all a matter of managing interest rates, creating programs of public works and welfare, while manipulating growing deficits.

So ran the accepted wisdom of the famous Columbia course in Contemporary Civilization during the years 1933 through 1935 when I went through it and it went through me and shattered much of the protective shell of nostalgic High Church ritualism that covered my attempted approach to clerical life.

During that period I had no knowledge of the potent Christian criticisms of this absurdly unreal view of history, even though right across the campus Reinhold Niebuhr was exposing the whole sham in the course of his lectures and writing at the Union Theological Seminary. Nor was I acquainted with Karl Barth's shattering critique of the pre-World War I liberal optimism that had marked both British and much European Protestant theology, especially in Germany. And I had never heard of the work of the great Anglican apologist and theologian, William Temple, whose notable book called *Nature, Man, and God* was later to influence my thinking. Most of the time, I was just confused, although I managed to cling to the battered vestiges of my religion—frequently with the help of Father George Ford.

I was not sure why, but I sensed that something was very wrong with the C.C. party line. Events in the real world, far from Morningside Heights, cast heavy shadows on the world that was supposedly still lighted by a rationalistic sun that had risen in the eighteenth century. There were cold, dark winds blowing across Germany, for example, which suggested that once again the barbarian tribes were moving restlessly and that a new Dark Age was a possibility. Contemporary civilization itself, which refused to conform to its Columbia portrait, may have denied heaven, but it appeared to be about to face the reality of what would be at least an earthly hell.

If, as young instructors such as Lionel Trilling and Jacques Barzun seemed to imply, traditional Christianity was either dead or dying, what appeared to be about to fill the void it was leaving behind? Might it not be best described in Yeats' poem "The Second Coming" in which he suggested that some nameless monster was about to appear in the world, rather than a new age of science, greater enlightenment, and plastic palaces for everyone? Horror was just over the horizon, even as the social science professors were in Washington creating the New Deal so that Americans could sing "Happy Days Are Here Again."

All over Europe since the great crash of the American economy in 1929, it was evident that liberal democracy was in almost total disarray. Enlightenment constitutions of the kind dreamed of by Woodrow Wilson had evaporated in Hungary, Spain, Portugal, Poland, Yugoslavia and Italy. In the very year I entered Columbia and began the course in Contemporary Civilization, Hitler took the oath as German Chancellor and the short-lived Weimar Republic died quietly. Purges and terror ruled in Stalin's version of the Worker's Paradise, and his prison camps were holding captive at least ten million—a population that grew ever greater as the purges mounted and what was left of Stalin's revolutionary comrades disappeared beneath the earth of Mother Russia.

For many of our instructors at Columbia it seemed, however, that Stalinism was really nothing more than necessary "democratic centralism" and was to be distinguished as such. Meanwhile Pilsudski in Poland, Primo de Rivera in Spain, and Metaxas in Greece were authoritarian dictators and war-mongering Fascists, as were their peers Hitler and Mussolini. Mussolini, in particular, was said to stand in sharp contrast to the peace-loving Stalin, as was abundantly clear from the Italian conquest of Ethiopia that was finally completed in 1936.

Of course, local echoes of all this and more echoed at Columbia. The *Nation* claimed that the University's Casa Italiana was a festering nest of Fascism, and the student Political Union debated whether or not such a thing should be tolerated on the campus or even near it. I recall that I was one of the speakers in favor of a policy of toleration. We also debated about whether or not Columbia should permit a visit from Dr. Hans Orth, who had been booked by the national Intercollegiate Council to explain the Nazi point of view on American campuses, provided that wherever he was permitted to speak there would be at least one other speaker engaged to refute what he said.

And there was much debate at the Political Union as to whether or not Communism offered a viable solution to the problems that continued to plague New Deal America, in spite of the best efforts of The Enlightened Ones from our very own faculty who had spent so much time in Washington. In these debates I had a great deal to say and proved how effective my C.C. indoctrination had been by arguing that capitalism deserved at least one more chance to save itself through the application of Keynesian management of the economy. There were, of course, those who suggested that such management was no management but rather the death of our sacred free market economy and even of our cherished democratic liberty.

Looking back at my Columbia days from the perspective of more than half a century, I have the impression that I was always talking, probably even in my sleep. Much of this talking was done on public platforms. I should note that I also sang on public platforms during my first year, when I was—as a former choir boy—a member of the Glee Club. At the major recitals—as when we joined the Barnard Glee Club and the University orchestra to do Brahms' German Requiem—we wore very formal white ties and tails. These garments served me well at any number of Barnard dances and helped by their dignity to cover my nervousness when my date had to go through the process of presenting me to the very formidable President of Barnard, Virginia C. Gildersleeve.

My enthusiasm for singing, however, did not last beyond my first year. What I most loved to do was to talk in public to whomever would listen. Naturally, I joined the debating team and eventually became its President in my Senior year. We debated with teams from many colleges and when we weren't doing that, we debated among ourselves. There was no political issue we would not discuss. Before an audience of conservative Masons, we argued that Roosevelt should not be re-elected, while Yale upheld the opposite position. Of course, since the decision was up to the audience, we won overwhelmingly. Before the Institute for Arts and Sciences we argued against Harvard that the United States should support the sanctions of the League of Nations against Italy because of Italy's invasion of Ethiopia. The audience that night voted that the debate was a tie. The Columbia and Harvard debating teams were about as effective as was the ineffective League of Nations on the Ethiopian question, but I thought that the tie vote was a victory for Harvard because they had to defend the more difficult proposition.

The most exciting event of my college debating experience was a radio debate with the Oxford Union, which was simultaneously broadcast by CBS in New York and the BBC. The stirring topic was whether or not governments should control the production of munitions. The British, characteristically, did not wish to seem to be wholly for or against; they requested what was called a "mixed" debate. Thus my friend and classmate Ben Brown was matched with the President of the Oxford Union, C.P. Mayhew, while I was joined as the partner of Patrick Anderson from Christ Church College. We argued for the private control of the weapons industry, a position that was then typically conservative and one with which I personally did not agree. Needless to say, there was no decision and the world went right on making its weapons as it had been doing since time immemorial.

In between talking in public and in endless "bull sessions" that extended far into many nights, I managed to attend classes with a reasonable degree of regularity. And I experienced some of the really great teachers of that period, such as Mark Van Doren, Raymond Weaver, and Irwin Edman. Van Doren was beyond a doubt the finest teacher— and one of the finest human beings—I have known. His very steady, very big, hands seemed to guide his classes with a gentle, firm control and a skill that seemed effortless only because he always had not only massive scholarship but also the power of creative critical insight, especially when he was leading a discussion of Shakespeare. And in the profession of teaching literature, where fads and fashions are always coming in or going out, Van Doren never failed to display the rather uncommon virtue of common sense.

For example, to a student who asked, "Do you think that

if Christopher Marlowe had lived longer, he would have been a better playwright than Shakespeare?" Van Doren answered with a quiet smile, "All I can say is that he didn't."

Edman's philosophy courses glowed with his truly humane spirit, once one overcame the impression that he looked like a myopic rabbit that had somehow lost its ears and was munching absent-mindedly on a piece of blackboard chalk which it had mistaken for a carrot. Chewing the chalk reflectively was something he did between moments of brilliant exposition. I studied aesthetics with him and got a feeling for Santayana's way of turning what is beautiful into a mode of knowing what is also a species of reality.

Edman's course called A Philosophical Examination of Christianity was a fascinating example of an attitude exemplified by Santayana's famous remark that there may very well not be a God but the Virgin Mary is most certainly His mother. We spent a fair amount of time on Pauline mysticism and then skipped to William James and discussions of the varieties of Christian religious experience. The major question on the final examination asked for what one might consider to be a meaningful statement of personal religious belief in the year 1937. My answer was to write out the Nicene Creed.

When grades were posted, I received not a grade but an Incomplete entry in my record. When I went to inquire about this, Professor Edman said, "I was sure you would come. I want to ask you a question. You did well during the term and wrote a good term paper, but having read your answer to the major essay question on the final, what I want to know is whether you really got anything out of this course at all."

As this episode illustrates, Columbia was not the sort of place in which those who did well in philosophy courses were expected to end up taking Christianity's traditional creeds very seriously. But Edman was consistently a liberal humanist and when he was convinced that I really meant what I had written and that I was not being flippant, he gave me an "A" in the course.

In addition to my being exposed to teachers like Edman and Van Doren, I was also very fortunate to be guided in my program of studies by the dean of the college, Herbert Hawkes. His professional academic discipline spoke in a language I have never been able to handle, for he was a mathematician. But his wisdom, being far greater than mine, surmounted this and any other obstacles between us. He, for example, wisely concluded that I would do better to study two sequential years of laboratory work in psychology rather than taking one year of physics or chemistry, in addition to the year I had spent amid the smells and microscopes of the world of botany.

He also steered me away from the most popular course in the college curriculum, which was William Cornell Casey's Introduction to Sociology. As a notable mathematician, Dean Hawkes rightly understood that sociology is mostly a statistical game in which numbers are manipulated to prove whatever the game player wants to prove about almost any social phenomenon. I have often had reason to be grateful to Dean Hawkes after reading some of the professional work of Andrew Greeley.

Of course, the main courses I took were in English literature and it was in one of them that I first discovered the voice of T.S. Eliot, whose oracular utterances in both verse and literary criticism were, at that time, thought to be quite remarkable. When, for example, Eliot announced that Milton's "Paradise Lost" was a failure, there were many academic people, as well as other serious readers, who believed him. Certainly, I did, for my youthful estimate of his position in the world of literary critical opinion was highly inflated.

But whatever his worth as a poet and critic may be, Eliot played a major role in my undergraduate life, for in the face of all that C.C. had to say about it, Eliot seemed to support my conviction that traditional Christianity, especially in its Anglican form, was vitally important. Eliot's "The Wasteland" described the world very much as I saw it. We were living in what was truly a spiritual wasteland that had its immediate origins in the devastation of World War I, in which well over ten million people, probably one third of whom were civilians, had lost their lives, as whole empires were swept away and the core of Western culture was badly battered.

In the early 1920's Eliot himself had been one of those who, as he wrote, believed that "the dissolution of value had in itself a positive value." But by 1928 he had undergone the change of outlook that is represented in his poem "Ash Wednesday" and in subsequent works he developed a line of thought which sustained my own reaction to the kind of thinking I had encountered in so many ways at Columbia. It was a viewpoint that he called "the Catholic philosophy of disillusion." It was skeptical regarding the pretensions of a purely secular culture. In his view, this skepticism arose from a deeper faith in the essential importance of what he called the values of Christianity, which included such things as "holy living and holy dying," sanctity, chastity, humility and austerity and a proper sense of the imperfection of human beings apart from their recognizing and responding to the saving grace of God mediated through Jesus Christ and the Church, which in former times he had described in a well-known poem as an old hippopotamus stuck in the mud.

In his Choruses from "The Rock," written in 1934, Eliot saw the Anglican Church in a very different light as that which was essential to a world of civility, but one had the feeling that he was not hopeful that it would really triumph over the forces of disintegration. I suppose it was Eliot's skepticism about the pretensions of utilitarian materialism and the sort of pragmatism I had found at Columbia that helped me most to remain in the Christian camp; the alternatives were made much less attractive by what Eliot had to say about them.

I was not enthusiastic about Eliot's statement in his preface "For Lancelot Andrewes" that he was an Anglo-Catholic in religion, a Tory in politics, and a classicist in art. I recall being in sympathy with a statement of John Strachey's that he could understand Eliot's being a Tory and a classicist. But Strachey suggested that if Eliot wanted to be a Catholic, he ought to become "a real one."

There were indeed times when I thought that I ought to become a "real one." Once, for a few months, I actually undertook a course of instruction with Father Ford, and I remember telling him that if I were received into the Church, it was likely that I would attempt to become a Jesuit. He feigned shock and said he hoped I would do no such thing. He suggested that I would probably make more progress as a Christian if I became a Franciscan.

I did not conceal my sympathy for the Catholic Church nor the fact that I was taking instructions from Bishop Washburn, but instead requested him to remove my name from the list of postulants for Holy Orders in view of my probable conversion to Catholicism. He did so in a very kind letter. As a consequence, however, I had to surrender my scholarship from the Society for Promoting Religion and Learning. But Dean Hawkes, always a good and understanding friend of undergraduates, managed to obtain another scholarship for me from the University which was of equal value and thus enabled me to remain in college.

That I did not then become a Catholic was largely due to

Father Ford's perception that my interest in the Church was mostly a rebellion against the secular humanism of the University. Had I been a student in a Catholic college, my rebellion would have been against Thomism. In any event, he advised me to wait and to do a great deal more reading in both Catholic and Anglican authors.

I took this advice and read such books as More and Cross's *Anglicanism*, with its fine treatment of seventeenth century High Church Anglican writers. I also read Butler's *Analogy* and Gore's *The Church and the Ministry*. Moreover, in Catholic Jacques Maritain's forceful discussion of Luther, Descartes, and Rousseau in his *Three Reformers*, I found not only reinforcement of Eliot's criticism of post-Enlightenment attitudes, but an introduction to a Christian philosophy of personalism, which gave an effective answer to the depersonalizing effects of modern mass culture in both democratic and totalitarian countries.

Moreover, I developed some personal friendships with certain Episcopalian priests in New York. John Golding at the Cathedral of St. John the Divine introduced me to the work of Kenneth Kirk, who was Bishop of Oxford and a notable scholar who wrote convincingly about Christian ethics, as well as the spiritual life. John was always available to students at Columbia and had a cordial relationship with Father Ford.

On several occasions I had the opportunity of meeting and talking at length with Niebuhr's wife Ursula, who was highly trained in Anglican theology and who struck me as far more brilliant in her calm British way of dealing with conflicting ideas than was her husband with his explosive Lutheran bombardment of the errors of the times.

Especially important was my coming to know Gordon Wadhams, who was rector of the Church of the Resurrection—an Anglo-Catholic center of worship and influence to

which a number of notable individuals had attached themselves. One of these was, for example, Frances Perkins, who
was Secretary of Labor and who periodically came up from
Washington to worship there.

Everything liturgical at the Church of the Resurrection
was self-consciously Roman in a ritual more or less overlaid
on the language of the *Book of Common Prayer*. Indeed over
thirty years later when Gordon had become a Roman Catholic priest and pastor of a parish in West Hartford, Connecticut, a friend from New York, seeing how Gordon had implemented the reforms of Vatican II, remarked that whereas the
Church of the Resurrection had exemplified the Roman rite
in an Anglican Church, Gordon's Catholic post-Vatican II
parish exemplified the Anglican rite in a Roman church.

Of course, in the days when I knew the group of Anglo-
Catholics at the Church of the Resurrection, if anyone had
suggested that the Roman Catholic Church would someday
authorize the use of vernacular liturgies, that opinion would
have been laughed out of court. What we wanted to do was
to return to the Latin, after the example of the Anglican Benedictine monks at Nashdom Abbey, where lived the notable
English liturgical scholar Dom Gregory Dix, whose work *The
Shape of the Liturgy* was widely acclaimed by Catholic
scholars.

By the academic year 1935–36 I was, however, more and
more taken up with matters of greater moment than liturgical languages.

I had become a student activist and had gone far beyond
mere debates about social issues. Thus I was involved in the
formation of the left-wing American Student Union in Columbus, Ohio; the annual student Anti-War Strike every
April 22; the New York May Day parades; protests against
racism, and efforts to improve the lot of the rural poor.

These and other similar causes seemed to be Christian

concerns. The Jewish prophets cried for social justice; Christ condemned wealth as an obstacle to salvation; the early Christians were said to have had held all their goods in common.

Could it not be that the goals of Communism had much to commend them? And were not the Communists evidently in the front line of battle for social and racial justice in America?

Looking for answers to such questions, I discovered that there were whole group of Anglican clergy in England who taught, much after the fashion of naive proponents of what is today called Liberation Theology, that one could accept the social analysis and political programs of Communism without embracing Marxian atheism. All this was explained at length in a volume called *Christianity and Social Revolution*, edited by Charles Raven, the Regius Professor of Divinity in the University of Cambridge. Contributors to this volume included John Macmurray, Grote Professor of Philosophy at the University of London and two parish vicars, Conrad Noel of Thaxted, Essex and Gilbert Clive Binyon, of Bilsdale, Yorkshire. Raven's Preface stated that the intention of the book was to show that Christianity is revolutionary; that Christianity has Communistic aspects; and that a synthesis of Communism and Christianity offers the best possible hope for the future. Macmurray argued that the people the Bible calls "the poor" are Communism's "wretched of the earth" and that we are to understand them to be those who in the final conflict of the apocalyptic Day of the Lord will be seen as the international proletariat that must inevitably rule the earth in a new age of justice and universal peace. Many of the ideas in this book were much later expressed by Hewlett Johnson, the so-called Red Dean of Canterbury, who was actually decorated by Stalin. The illusions of Liberation Theology are nothing new. There are those today who, like the very misguided Vicar of Bilsdale, write that the primitive Church's revolutionary character was subverted by Constantine, who turned the Church into an instrument of the ruling class. This is, of course, a gross over-simplification of history, but one can understand how a clergyman of the Church of England might see the role of religion as being under the domination of a sovereign and a ruling class. All he would have to do would be to look around him.

In any case, I bought the thesis of the Anglican liberation theologians of 1936 and, having managed to persuade Bishop Washburn to restore me to postulancy for Holy Orders, set about finding a way to work with the Communists that I knew on campus so as to show them that real Christianity was not an oppressive but a liberating force.

It seemed that the time was right because the Communists everywhere were then following what they called a United Front Policy under which they were, they said, prepared to unite with all those opposed to the evils of war and Fascism. Even the Columbia chapter of the Young Communist League, known as the Y.C.L., which was anything but a united front organization, went so far as to assure me that I could join even though I did not accept the atheism of Marx.

Thus I eagerly joined the Y.C.L. at Columbia and characteristically refused to have my membership kept secret, like that of every other member. Instead, I agreed to be the open spokesman for the group on campus.

There were obvious risks in this, as I quickly discovered when in May, 1936 President Butler accepted an invitation from the University of Heidelberg to send an official representative of the University to take part in the Nazi celebration of Heidelberg's five hundredth anniversary. The Young Communists took the lead in planning a protest and the Columbia chapter of the American Student Union, guided by other Young Communists and by myself as spokesman, publicly demanded that the acceptance of the Nazi invitation be rescinded at once.

This demand was ignored. Consequently, on the night of May 12 a noisy demonstration was held on South Field. About two hundred students gave Nazi salutes there as a great book-burning bonfire was lighted. I impersonated Professor Arthur F.H. Remy. who was to represent Columbia at the Nazi celebration. Another student represented Hitler and threw books into the flames to symbolize the barbarism of the Nazi intolerance of people and ideas that opposed them. One of these books was the *New York Telephone Directory*, which was condemned by the student impersonating Hitler because it contained so many Jewish names. After the book-burning a mock honorary degree was given to "the distinguished Columbia representative" for recognizing the culture and civilization of the Nazis.

Students then performed a snake dance around the fire and bearing signs such as "Butler Diddles While Books Burn," poured out of the campus to march on Dr. Butler's residence on Morningside Heights, where some elderly and wealthy benefactors of the University were being entertained at dinner. As usual I made a speech, this time on the steps of the President's house. So did a sophomore named Robert Burke, a rugged boxer who came from a steel-worker background and knew how to use the vigorous language of confrontation, which he proceeded to do to the great delight of the crowd. Someone then nominated President Butler for election to the Reichstag and, after a loud chorus of aye's the crowd dispersed.

The next morning I was, not surprisingly, summoned to the office of the good Dean Hawkes, who informed me that the demonstration had gone beyond the bounds of good taste and decent, civilized behavior when it invaded President Butler's privacy. Moreover, he described Bob Burke's speech as "rowdy, abusive, and violent." I replied that it had not seemed so to me. The Dean said that in his view apologies were in order, not for the protest itself but for the personal affront to the President and his guests at dinner in his private residence. A week later I wrote a public letter of apology for any discourtesy that had taken place at President Butler's home. To the best of my knowledge Burke did not do so. The consequence was that he was expelled from the University. I did not know it at the time but Professor Harry Carman, who later became Dean, informed me that when the time came, I was refused admission to Phi Beta Kappa because of my own part in the protest at the President's house.

That summer of 1936 I did something which, on the face of it, seemed totally inconsistent with my radical reputation on campus. I enrolled in the Platoon Leaders Class for college men that was conducted by the U.S. Marine Corps at Quantico, Virginia. My thinking was not unlike that of the Catholic liberation theologians who have expressed their willingness to use force in the cause of what they call "peace and justice." The Spanish Civil War was evidence enough that starry-eyed writers, poets and professors were not of much use fighting against professional soldiers on the Fascist side. Indeed one of my acquaintances, Mike Papas, had died as a member of the ragged forces on the Loyalist side. Mike was a track star, but he knew very little about the use of weapons. The way the world was going, it seemed to me, showed that war with Germany was inevitable. Spain was obviously a bloody dress rehearsal. The thing for friends of freedom to do was to learn to fight. And who knew more about fighting than the Marines. There was no better school for prospective warriors.

I have many times had reason to thank God for my decision to join the Platoon Leaders Class, where I learned much more than the use of small bore weapons and close order drill. My company commander was a most unusual professional Marine. He was Evans Carlson, a man whose first-hand knowledge of the Chinese Communists helped him to create the Marine Raider Battalions of World War II. Having listened to him I had no doubt whatever that the Chinese Communists would one day not only rule China but become the teachers of guerilla warfare to much of the suppressed world. But more importantly, he and his enlisted aids formed a faculty that taught well the lessons of discipline, physical courage, and integral personal honor which had been conspicuously missing in my education.

When I returned to the Columbia campus in the fall, the term began with a series of futile efforts to get Bob Burke reinstated. I had been elected a member of the Student Board for my Senior year, but the majority of the members of that body refused to join my two Southern liberal friends—Ben Brown and Jim Dunaway—in supporting a resolution calling upon Dean Hawkes to reverse his decision on Burke.

But our battle over the Heidelberg affair had not been altogether in vain. In that my final year at the University it was learned that Columbia had received another Nazi invitation. This time it was to be represented at the two-hundredth anniversary celebration at Gottingen. President Butler refused this invitation and issued a characteristically pompous statement in which he praised the former excellence of German science and scholarship and expressed the hope that it would someday be restored. Perhaps this was his way of apologizing to his own students for the indecency of his acceptance of the Heidelberg invitation on behalf of their university. But I suspect that he merely wanted to avoid further disturbances.

The summer with the Marines had helped me to take a

realistic look at myself and what I had been doing. I realized that I had been used as a front person in the Heidelberg affair and I saw very clearly that Liberation Theology which tries to make a synthesis of Christianity and Marxism is nonsense. In any such attempted alliance, the poor Christians would eventually find themselves providing dinner for the Marxist lions in the arena of political conflict. Moreover, factionalism, which has always been the hallmark of radical parties, emerged within the Young Communist League members on campus. It became apparent to me that on any scale of action the Communist struggle for power would not be a struggle to give power to "the people" but rather to obtain power for those who could best manipulate them.

Consequently, I finally wrote a letter to the *Columbia Spectator* in which I publicly terminated my personal version of the United Front by announcing my resignation from the Young Communist League. I guess that in so doing I became one of what would be a long procession of those who turned away from Communism in the coming years. For many the whole Marxist promise of peace and justice became what has been called "the god that failed."

My God, however, did not fail, for my God was not Marxism but the God Whose Son redeems the world. During my senior year I was very active in church-related social action groups and learned a great deal about the real fighters for justice in America when I worked with a youth group at St. Martin's Episcopal Church in Harlem.

That year, too, I listened more and more to the poets whose work I was reading in courses or in the company of friends. Eliot continued to be my mentor but so did Auden and many others, especially Yeats, who was more and more seen as the best of the modern lot. And I wrote in imitation of the poets I liked, as did so many others among my friends and acquaintances, among whom were John Berryman,

Ralph Toledano, J. Treville Latouche, Boris Todrin, Leonard
Robinson, Barry Ulanov, and dear, scholarly, kindly Milton
Crane.

And then there was Tom Merton, editor-in-chief of the
yearbook, the *Columbian*; art editor of *Jester*, the humor
magazine; and cross-country runner. He was never, to the
best of my recollection, an active member of the Philolexian
Society, the oldest college literary society in America, where
student poets met to read their works aloud and to insult
one another. Perhaps he did not care to be insulted by those
he sometimes seemed to see as less gifted than he was. Perhaps wisely, he preferred to submit to the criticism of Mark
Van Doren, whose protege he was said to be.

I was President of the Philolexian during my Senior year
and a close friend of some of its members. I was never close
to Tom Merton, whom I rather disliked and certainly envied
for his relationship to Mark Van Doren. In those days there
was no evidence that Tom would become a world-famous
monk, a poet and writer on mysticism, to say nothing of a
household word in certain Catholic circles. He was, as he so
well pictures himself in his justly admired *Seven Storey Moun-
tain*, and he seemed to me to be sophisticated beyond his
years in matters of paper and ink.

As I think of how distant we were from one another then
and of how, in the strange Providence of God, we both—
most improbably—became such different kinds of Catholic
priests, I am once more reminded that with God it is never
safe to say, "Never."

The class that graduated from Columbia in 1937 voted its
senior year as its best year. For me, it certainly was so. My
life appeared to be finally moving in its direction towards the
goal with which I had first come to Columbia. Naturally,
however, this was not without its complications, for I had
developed what is now called a relationship with a Barnard

student and we were talking about marriage. And there was the old question in my mind as to whether or not marriage and Anglo-Catholic priesthood were compatible ideas. But that issue did not have to be resolved in June of 1937.

There were a lot of things, like thoughts of the continuing Great Depression and the probability of a future war, that all of us put aside as we prepared to celebrate commencement. A poll of the class showed that we chose Benny Goodman as the leader of the best dance band and Vassar—certainly not Barnard—as our favorite women's college. Sex, not religion or politics, was voted the favorite topic of conversation, and it may well have been so, for it was also a favorite activity. Contrary to what the sociologists say in their systems of numerology, the so-called sexual revolution did not begin after World War II but much before it. The members of the class hoped the Depression would end soon, but expected another big financial crash in ten years. Meanwhile, Jack Benny was our favorite radio entertainer.

That, in general, was the frame of mind in which we left behind our study of contemporary civilization and departed Morningside Heights where the young lions had roared at a world which was soon to become even more of a jungle than they knew.

THREE

The Parson's Handbook

When I emerged from Columbia I was what some Episcopalian clerical circles would describe as a "spike," which meant a person whose religious opinions were narrow, rigid, and terminated by a very sharp, very defensive point. This point was the notion that the English Reformation, like Protestantism in general, was a cultural disaster that was now all but dead. Accordingly, Anglo-Catholics represented not only a recovery from this disaster but also a movement to return to some sort of corporate reunion with Rome in which Anglican identity would be recognized and given its rightful place under papal authority. In Britain this theory was represented by a publication called by its Anglo-Catholic editors *Reunion*. On the front cover of each issue appeared the triple crown and the crossed keys, which symbolized papal authority.

"Spikes" were, of course, very defensive because they were very insecure in the anomalous position of claiming to be Catholics while continuing to adhere to what everyone else recognized as one of the most respectably Protestant denominations. The incongruity of this clearly had its humor-

ous aspects, which did not escape the attention of a delightful curmudgeon, the Reverend Alexander Cummings, who
lived in Poughkeepsie, New York and published a magazine
known as the *Chronicle*. This often very witty publication
trumpeted like an elephant that it represented the vast majority of the members of what was, after all, officially The
Protestant Episcopal Church in the United States of America,
sometimes referred to as P.E.C.U.S.A. It had great fun reporting the bizarre doings of the Anglo-Catholic clergy in
their attempts to imitate Roman Catholic rituals. A column
was devoted to a fictional lady known as "your Anglo-Catholic aunt," who was pictured as visiting parishes like the
Church of the Resurrection, which was described as being
located "but a mere biretta's throw from the subway." What
this fictional lady saw in such places was satirized very
cleverly, and the fact was that Anglo-Catholic rectors in the
New York area did not feel that they had really been properly recognized as such unless they had been written up in
the *Chronicle*.

The position of the "spikes" was made very awkward by
the simple fact that Anglicanism is, as has often been noted,
not a very happy synthesis but rather a constantly discordant
juxtaposition of opposites dating back to the character imposed upon the Church of England under the political com-
promises of the Elizabethan establishment of its place in official English life. The "spikes" found themselves to be the
very unhappy opposites of their fellow Anglicans, whose
loosely joined church structures disturbed few and who answered charges of inconsistency in their teaching by saying
that life escapes logic. After all did not the British monarch,
who is the Supreme Head of the Church of England and by
law necessarily Protestant, preside regularly over all sorts of
medieval pageantry filled with symbols of regal power while
actually being virtually powerless? Why then should not the

royal Church from time to time look somewhat Catholic and medieval while being in reality a national symbol of the Establishment at prayer?

I think it was Shelley who once described the Archbishop of Canterbury as "the King's Minister for Celestial Affairs"—a symbolic figure in a royal mythology and recognized as such by sensible people. Why would anyone, except a few misguided Anglo-Catholics, really worry about the question of whether or not this stately prelate was really an archbishop—like Roman Catholics claimed to have? Such a discussion would be as fruitless as asking whether the reigning sovereign was really a monarch. In the very pragmatic modern world, where it was evident that the British constitutional system worked, questions about whether titles meant what they merely symbolized for ceremonial occasions were irrelevant. Sensible people understood such things.

Certainly, Bishop Washburn was a very sensible person. As he considered me among his postulants for Holy Orders, he must have concluded that since it was obvious that I was a "spike," I was not, at that stage of my development, a sensible person at all. But he seems to have made the very charitable judgment that I had the potential to become one and to find the "very real place" that there was for sensible High Church clergy in the very comprehensive world of the American version of Anglicanism, which was, after all, not any longer part of a mythology of Royal Establishment. Consequently, he prudently and firmly directed me to seek admission to the Berkeley Divinity School in New Haven, a seminary that was not known to be identified with any particular point of view or theology then known to be current in the Episcopal Church.

I had not so much as heard of the Berkeley Divinity School. I had fully expected to attend the General Theological Seminary in New York, some of whose faculty I had met. That institution, however, had a somewhat High Church reputation, rather like that of the Cathedral of St. John the Divine under Bishop William Thomas Manning. Bishop Washburn, I think quite correctly, felt that this was not a place for me to grow into a sensible young parson.

There were a number of Episcopalian seminaries of which I had heard but did not consider. There was, for example, one in Virginia, which was conservative, Low Church, and very Virginian. Some said that there was actually a shrine on the campus dedicated to Robert E. Lee. Then there was the Episcopal Theological School in Cambridge, a place of genteel tradition, association with Harvard and vagueness of outlook, which went under the general description of being Broad Church and seeking to bring Christianity "into line with twentieth century thought." And then there was a seminary way out in the hinterlands of the land beyond the Hudson River. It was called Nashotah House, a name which suggested an Indian reservation to me. It was known, of course, as a perfect breeding ground for "spikes" and had the reputation of being very, very Anglo-Catholic in its devotional piety, but possibly a bit short with respect to its scholarship. In any case, even if I had wanted to journey so far away from what I regarded as civilization, Bishop Washburn, as a sensible man, would never have permitted it.

At his behest, therefore, I went to the Berkeley Divinity School, not knowing anything about it but consoling myself with the thought that New Haven was not far from New York and the knowledge that the libraries and certain other facilities of Yale were available to Berkeley Divinity students.

Thus Berkeley's academic resources were far greater than one might have thought upon first encountering its disparate collection of aging buildings near the lower end of

Prospect Street on land now occupied by the Yale Hockey Rink. Up the hill on Prospect was the conglomorate of Yale Divinity School, significantly quite removed from the center of things and looking for all the world like an attempt to reproduce in miniature the appearance of the University of Virginia.

Indeed, imitations of most traditional forms of Western architecture stood cheek by jowl on the sprawling, scattered properties of Yale. The Gothic gymnasium was known to some as St. Calisthenic's Cathedral, while the main circulation desk of the Sterling Library looked rather like the high altar of a great medieval abbey surrounded by chapels and confessionals, which were really alcoves where the card catalogues were housed. From the window of my room in the seedy old Berkeley dormitory, I looked out over a cemetery where generations of Connecticut Yankees slept undisturbed behind what was evidently a wall and great gate intended to represent the defenses of some ancient Egyptian ruler.

Looking out at that scene one wintery afternoon, a classmate from Moosehead Lake in Maine asked me if I knew why New England Yankees were like potatoes. His answer to this question was, "The best part of 'em is underground."

Living evidence that this statement was not entirely accurate was Berkeley's Dean, the Very Reverend William Palmer Ladd, who had joined the faculty in 1904 and who, in 1937, had been Dean for nineteen years. The school itself, with its roots deep in the Episcopal Diocese of Connecticut, had been originally located in Middletown, where Dean Ladd had received the degree of Doctor of Divinity from Wesleyan University in 1919. But he had also earned a reputation for being a man whose political views were a bit too radical for the taste of most people in Middletown.

Born in the hills of Lancaster, New Hampshire in 1870, the Dean had studied at Philips Andover to prepare for

Dartmouth, where he graduated in 1891. He then took a tour abroad, which accounted for his very cosmopolitan sense of the universe of scholars. A lifelong admirer of the great Erasmus, Dean Ladd had, in the best tradition of the humanists of the Renaissance, sampled university life in Europe during the 1890s at Leipzig, Paris, and finally at Oxford. That was a truly vintage time for the European and English universities, a time of great civility that has never been recaptured. The young William Ladd drank it all in, and although he certainly never lost the flavor of rural New Hampshire, he was always and everywhere much at home among scholars.

The Berkeley Divinity School, as I knew it, was really his creation. It had been named for Bishop George Berkeley, the same eighteenth century philosopher who had so much influenced Columbia's first President. But Berkeley's strange notion that we know only that reality which is perceived in our consciousness was apparently not a part of Dean Ladd's thinking. He was too much of a Yankee for that and probably agreed with the words attributed by Boswell to Dr. Johnson, who, speaking of Berkeley's philosophy, kicked a big rock and exclaimed, "Thus do I refute him."

But when the Dean decided to move his divinity school out of provincial Middletown years before I knew the place, he was shrewd enough to recall that Bishop Berkeley, during a sojourn in Newport, Rhode Island from 1728 to 1731, had donated a substantial number of books to the then-fledgling Yale College. Coming with his Berkeley Divinity School to New Haven and proximity to Yale, the Dean's plan was to have a relationship with the University like that of its theological houses of studies to Oxford. He reminded Yale of its ancient debt to Bishop Berkeley and eventually gained the kind of affiliation he desired.

Thus Berkeley was a unique sort of place where faculty

and students had access to Yale classes and facilities within the University while Berkeley maintained its own special identity, which was powerfully affected by the special role Connecticut had played in the creation of a form of Anglican Christianity that appeared after the American Revolution as the Protestant Episcopal Church in the United States of America.

After the Revolution, although thirty-five of the fifty-six signers of the Declaration of Independence were, at least in name, members of the Church of England, there was much talk of abolishing Anglicanism in the new country because it was seen as royalist and therefore subversive of the new republic. Moreover, there were no Anglican bishops in America to ordain priests, and the clergymen who had been ordained in England were suspect as men who had not hesitated to swear allegiance to the hated George III, who was, of course, the Supreme Head of the Church of England.

Under such unfavorable circumstances two clergymen, William White of Philadelphia and Samuel Seabury of Connecticut led the effort to create a form of Anglicanism that was suited to the new nation. White claimed that if anyone was consecrated as a bishop in England, he would obviously not be acceptable because of the matter of the Royal Supremacy. For this reason White was prepared to opt for a Presbyterian ordination rite, but Seabury and the Connecticut forces insisted that to have continuity with Anglicanism it would be necessary to have bishops. They were, in other words, stalwart Episcopalians.

Seabury was finally consecrated as a bishop, not in England but in Scotland where the Scottish bishops of the Episcopal Church of Scotland had refused to swear allegiance to the Hanoverian kings and were called non-jurors. Thus Seabury was able to bring Anglican episcopacy to America cleansed of all royalist taint. Actually, he was a former Tory who had served as a chaplain for British troops during the Revolution. But he managed to live that down and in developing Anglicanism in Connecticut, was able to stand up against his Congregationalist opponents, who belonged to the church of the majority in the state, where Congregationalism was, for all intents and purposes, the official religion.

Thus the Berkeley Divinity School, which had in its chapel a very plain little wooden altar purportedly once used by Seabury, came out of a history which made it distinctly Episcopalian. Bishop Washburn had described the school as precisely an American Episcopalian divinity school, with a strong but unpretentious sense of relationship to the Anglican Communion of which it was a tiny part.

This description was, in fact, quite accurate, for Dean Ladd, who taught Church history, held that all existing evidence showed that episcopal polity had been and was essential to the Church and its ministry. There he stood firmly with Seabury and the Connecticut tradition. As for awareness of being within the Anglican Communion, every year there was another clergyman of the Church of England who had been designated as English Lecturer and had agreed to teach a course at Berkeley.

As a consequence, I was exposed to such teachers as Headmaster Neville Gorton, who later became Bishop of Coventry, and Cyril Hudson, a Canon of St. Albans. Canon Hudson in particular was quintessentially Church of England, with a proper British respect for tradition but a suspicion that Anglo-Catholics were too much given to the imitation of what he regarded as the degenerate liturgical fashions of Rome.

His sensibilities in this regard came to the surface one Sunday at the Church of St. Mary the Virgin in New York, where he had been scheduled to deliver the sermon at what was called High Mass. As I have observed earlier, St. Mary's was the very height of Anglo-Catholic dramatic ritual. At the Sunday High Mass there was always a great opening procession complete with gorgeous banners, vast quantities of incense, elaborately vested clergy and truly magnificent music. On the day of Canon Hudson's preaching engagement, he was, of course, placed in a position of prominence and walked beside the rector, as the procession wound its way around the aisles of the large church, with its participants at times almost obscured by the great clouds of incense coming from three thuribles, each swung by a tall altar server dressed in a flowing alb and wearing white gauntlets. Then there was a moment of silence, as the organist paused briefly before beginning another hymn. In the midst of this quiet, most of the congregation were startled to hear Cyril Hudson's hearty British voice as he turned to the rector beside him and said, "I say, old man, do you really do this sort of thing every Sunday?"

It was abundantly clear from his tone that this "sort of thing" was not the Canon's cup of tea, either here in America where it was a bit outlandish or in England where it was a most unpatriotic aping of "the Italian mission"—his way of referring to Roman Catholicism. He preferred a much plainer and more relaxed ecclesiastical atmosphere, in which one might be as comfortable as an old shoe. On one occasion, for example, he stood up to preach after Evening Prayer in the very plain little seminary chapel. He announced a Biblical text in the prophet Habakkuk by chapter and verse, but when he looked down to read it, discovered that it was not to be found at the place he had cited. He simply looked up pleasantly and said, "Apparently not, but no matter." Then, quite undisturbed, he went on to preach very well on the text he had failed to locate.

In addition to the English lecturers there were many other unusual visitors at Berkeley. The entire student body numbered about twenty-five so that they could all assemble in a large room in the big deanery. There almost every Sunday evening we students were expected to be present for what was called a "conversazione." This meant that some prominent person, who had probably unsuspectingly accepted an invitation to dinner, suddenly found folding doors opening after the meal to disclose a music room full of theological students who were encouraged to ask them questions. Even Eleanor Roosevelt was not spared this experience when she visited her friends the Ladds. But Eleanor was more than equal to the occasion.

In addition to the Dean, the English Lecturers, and a variety of distinguished visitors, some of whom stayed for extended periods, we were, of course, instructed by the regular faculty of four or five. And at Yale Divinity School we studied with such Protestant luminaries as Richard Niebuhr, Robert Calhoun, and Roland Bainton.

Our faculty, like the faculty at Yale Divinity, taught in the more or less conventional manner with which I had been well acquainted at Columbia. But in our first year at Berkeley, my seven classmates and I encountered the Dean's course in Ante-Nicene Church History, which was, to say the least, different. There were no textbooks; there were no lectures. There were, however, huge reading assignments in the original sources for the period before 325 and we quickly became quite painfully familiar with, for example, the Apostolic Fathers: Clement of Rome, Ignatius of Antioch, and Justin the Martyr. The class would begin with a laconic question or remark on the part of the Dean, but the rest of it was a kind of Socratic dialogue and God help the student who made any statement he could not document from the assigned primary sources. All of these sources were, of course, read in translation, which was a concession the Dean said he had to make to the hopeless illiteracy of those who could not read patristic Greek or Latin.

Thanks to the year of Greek I had taken at Columbia and thanks to my four years of Latin in high school, I was not altogether ignorant in the eyes of the Dean. And I had no difficulty with the course in the Greek New Testament, which one of our faculty offered at Yale, but which few took.

The three-year course in New Testament writings which we all took at Berkeley was dominated by the so-called Form Criticism first developed by Martin Dibelius. It appeared to be based on the premise that the "meaning" of what one read in the New Testament really depended heavily upon the literary form it happened to have been given. This notion, derived from linguistics and from formalist theories of literary criticism, now seems to be naive to literary critics who have reached the point of sophistication called "post-structuralism," which holds that the very stability of texts must be questioned since all verbal signs are unreliable and the notion of transcendental meaning is fiction.

Form criticism, it seemed, was saying that much of the traditional understanding of the themes of the New Testament was the result of the shaping of literary forms. One was given the impression that New Testament scholars alone were competent to decide what, if any, of the gospel texts actually reported an historical saying of Jesus. Indeed we were told that in the forests of German textual criticism there was emerging someone named Bultmann, who was in the process of expurgating the gospels of all their "mythological content," which, with the exception of the Passion narratives, was a great deal. We were offered little or nothing in the way of criticism of the German biblical critics. What was essentially missing was what ought to have been obvious, which is that the numerous schools of the critics from Reimarus on down generally say what they say because of prior theological presuppositions which limit their horizons.

As for our study of the Hebrew scriptures, it was tedious

and literally led us through deserts of archaeological studies of primitive Hebrew religious development. Of course, we had to mark our Bibles with crayons to delineate the supposed basic documents of the first five books, according to the theories of the German orientalist Julius Wellhausen, whose critical theories were, I understand, taken more seriously then than now. Of course, we read Gunkel on the Psalms, discovered that there were three Isaiahs, and read the prophets as men circumscribed by the times in which they lived.

Scripture studied in this fashion inevitably divorced supposed fact from religious faith and never managed to bring about any reconciliation between them. Such basic Christian beliefs as the Virgin Birth of Jesus, the historical fact of his rising from the dead, and the descent of the Holy Spirit upon the Apostles at Pentecost were seen, at best, as matters of ecclesiastical tradition and personal belief. There was really nothing in the Scripture courses that could possibly be of any use to an average parson engaged in developing either faith or intelligent understanding among his parishoners.

The preaching of the Good News was what we were supposed to learn from our course in homiletics, taught by a socially charming cleric, who had for many years had the pleasant task of presiding over the American Episcopal Church, which served what must have been a rather exclusive group of diplomatic families, American business types, and occasional tourists in Paris. He had a mellow voice that flowed gently, somewhat like honey, over any audience. And he was adept at teaching the art of a variety of preaching that soothes people without putting them asleep. The point was, we were told, to give people a pleasant experience that would "give them a lift" for their daily living.

Very different was the approach of the Dean, who had the most unenviable task of listening to the practice sermons of the young products of the homiletics course. Himself a very undistinguished preacher, the Dean was nonetheless a caustic critic, as he had to endure our pathetic efforts. I recall one occasion when he had to sit through one of my compositions, which was, in typical Anglo-Catholic fashion, loaded with references to various Church fathers and other ancient theologians. At the end, the Dean's very accurate comment was, "That was not a sermon; it was the Litany of the Saints."

At Berkeley it often seemed that the Dean was really like a primitive bishop who had gathered his students for ordination around him so that he might instruct them himself. This was nowhere more the case than when he attempted to teach Pastoral Theology. Like most seminary teachers of that subject, he knew almost nothing about it. Consequently, his classes were not based upon his own very limited experience of parish work but upon one of his favorite books, *The Parson's Handbook*, by Percy Dearmer, the British Vicar of Primrose Hill. Dearmer was a cleric who was considered to be most eccentric in a professional group that abounds in eccentrics. His book was replete with such arcane matters as the best way to "beat the bounds of the parish on Rogation Days" with willow or other tree branches while praying for a good harvest—a practice which must have begun in pre-Christian Anglo-Saxon times.

In his book, Dr. Dearmer was pictured arrayed in what was described as the costume of an Anglican priest "in official habit." The photograph showed him as a very striking, grey-haired figure wearing a "wrap-around" cassock, a Geneva gown, a Tudor-style "square cap" and a black scarf or tippet. I was later told in England that Dearmer had actually worn this outfit as he wandered about the streets of Primrose Hill and that on one occasion when he had been mocked by some street urchins, he had turned to them with these words, "Young Englishmen, I would have you know that this is the very same costume in which Thomas Cranmer and other English martyrs went to the stake." What the boys made of this allusion to the Protestant leaders executed in the time of the Catholic Queen Mary has not been recorded.

In any event, the Dearmer book purported to show that there was a distinctly Anglican way of conducting liturgical worship. The book told us nothing about parish administration, but devoted much space to praising and recommending the so-called Sarum Use of the Cathedral of Salisbury as the proper source and guide for truly Anglican worship. This Sarum Use, once attributed to St. Osmond, was an adaptation of the Roman liturgy to whatever British tastes may have been in the eleventh century. It seemed to me, at least, to have little to do with twentieth century parish life in the United States, even though it may have had some influence upon the *Book of Common Prayer* as it was first developed by the Reformers in 1549.

Fortunately, Dean Ladd took us far beyond Dearmer in a course which he offered in History of Liturgy. While visiting Germany during various summers, he had developed an acquaintance with the Benedictine monks of Maria Laach, which was a center for the then slowly developing phenomenon known as the Liturgical Movement in Roman Catholicism. At Maria Laach, under the direction of the scholarly Abbot Ildefonsus Herrwegen, a liturgical yearbook was published, and various changes, such as the use of the vernacular, were promoted.

I vividly recall listening to the Dean telling us that one day Roman Catholics would have their Mass in the vernacular instead of the Latin universally in use, with few special exceptions for Eastern rites, as was then the case. This struck me as a most unlikely and most undesirable development, and I said to the Dean, after class, that I was certain Rome would never allow any such thing. He smiled engimatically and simply said, "Let's wait and see." I have, of course, long since learned not to make positive predictions about what Rome would or would not allow.

Few things have had more of an influence upon my life than the Dean's admiration for the liturgical work that was being done by the scholarship and zeal of the monks of Maria Laach. I am certain that the Providence of God brought about the totally unexpected series of events that brought some of these men to the little world of our small divinity school in New Haven in the academic year of 1938–39. At that time, the future of monasticism in Germany under the Nazis was so uncertain and the possibility of war so real that several of the Beuron and Maria Laach monks came to the United States in order to look for a place to begin a new monastic foundation.

The Dean offered them help and also hospitality. Consequently, in a turn of events unheard of at that time we had a group of German Benedictines as guests during some of that school year. What was more they gave a series of lectures on the Roman Liturgy which were truly memorable. We students, of course, had really no idea that we were being instructed by some of the very finest of teachers in Dom Leo von Rudlof and Dom Damasus Winzen. I recall that a lecture by the learned theologian and former Prior, Dom Thomas Michel lasted almost two hours and seemed to have taken less than half that time. It was not only a brilliant academic performance but a profoundly religious experience; it was on the Holy Spirit, who was most surely present among all who were privileged to be there.

In the years to come I never forgot the way in which the faculty at Berkeley and at Yale Divinity School seemed to me to be so flat and essentially one-dimensional in contrast to the intellectual and spiritual depth of those Benedictine monks, who so effectively represented "the real thing."

To the Benedictine tradition we students owed something

else which we appreciated less than we did the teaching of
the monks. The Holy Rule of Benedict called for manual labor as something that was helpful to the life of the spirit. The
Dean agreed with the Holy Rule on this point. He was, in
addition, a shrewd Yankee and thus managed to cite the
Rule in support of his very practical way of getting students
to do manual work on the school property—work which,
had it been done by employees, would have cost money.

The Dean, who himself had married and had several
handsome children, nonetheless professed the highest regard for monasticism. He would, for example, describe such
things as the lack of heat in the chapel, where in winter one
could sometimes see one's breath at Matins, as something
very salutary and in the great monastic tradition of St. Bede,
who, the Dean said, lived to a great age as a saint and scholar
in the ancient northern monastery of Yarrow, without the
benefit of central heating.

Like the Dean, I also was attracted to monasticism. Even as
a Columbia undergraduate I had paid several visits to the
Episcopalian Monastery of the Holy Cross at West Park, New
York.

Upon returning from there on one occasion, I had written
a poem which appeared in *The Columbia Review* for May,
1937:

I know where mountains stand about the Rood,
The heaped clay, the sanctuary light
Are ringed by everlasting Might.
The beam I know of sharpened pain once hewed;
Whose sweated couch it was, I know His grace
Rests gently on the silent place.

I knew a tree-traced river where I heard
A thousand candled Aves' full devotion;
The plainsong of the sunlit motion

Sang the primal glory of the Word.
I knew a nameless thirst that I must slake;
I know a vow that I must take.

I took no such vow. In fact, it was about that time in my
college career that I began a relationship with a young woman at Barnard, to which I have referred earlier. We came to
consider ourselves engaged to marry and the relationship
lasted all during my three years at Berkeley, as well as for
some months after that time. It was a sometimes stormy affair, which caused both of us a good deal of pain, largely
because of my self-centered problems and persistent doubts
as to whether I should ever marry anyone.

While at Berkeley, I became attracted not so much to the
monastic life, hinted at in my poem, but to the celibate life of
a parish priest, as I saw this exemplified in Father William
Kibitz in the Anglo-Catholic parish of Christ Church, set in
the midst of the Yale campus area and attended by such distinguished members of the English faculty as Professors Tin-
ker and Pottle, the famous Boswell scholars. Bill Kibitz
served as a curate in the parish. He was a graduate of Berkeley and of St. Stephen's House, the Anglo-Catholic theological college at Oxford. I contrasted his life with that of
the rector, who was a married man.

Just as I had seen the professional Marines at Quantico as
being an elite breed, so it seemed to me that the celibate
clergy made their married counterparts look second-rate.
Bill Kibitz, for example, was as Gordon Wadhams had been,
available to those who needed him twenty-four hours a day.
He was not divided between the concerns of the priesthood
and the often pressing concerns of a family. Having no offspring, Bill did not have to worry about what the world
might think of his children. Nor did he have children who
were constantly in the parish spotlight and who became

neurotic as a consequence. As the daughter of one married Anglican parson once told me, she grew up with the constant feeling that she was "the rector's daughter who shouldn't oughta." Moreover, I observed that in helping parishoners with marital problems, Bill was never distracted by having a few of his own. He never had to say anything like what a married English vicar said to me many many years later, as we both sat at breakfast in a vast old vicarage from which his large family had all gone on holiday, "This truly reminds one of the old hymn, 'Peace, perfect peace, with loved ones far away.'"

I think that one can detect a certain undercurrent of uneasiness about mixing married and clerical life in various spots in the Anglican world, however small and isolated they may be. The fact is that Queen Elizabeth was very ambivalent on the subject and refused to receive the wives of her Reformation bishops at court. A tradition of celibacy, for example, remained among some university clerical dons, and one recalls that the young Anglican Newman early determined upon a celibate life. Being aware of this, I should not be at all surprised to find that in the American Episcopal Church of today, with its priestesses, there might not even be found females among the clerics who would much prefer a single life-style, as it might now be called, to that of their domesticated sisters in the cloth. And in some cases this might even be related to issues of the spiritual life.

As for my own class at Berkeley, three of the eight members were married men, whom the rest of us never came to know very well, and one was a full-blooded Sioux named Andrew Weston, who was, as far as I know, among the unmarried. But he kept his own counsel. When we graduated, although we were so few in numbers, it was a truly clerical event, for three of the graduates made speeches.

Looking back on that occasion, I find some significance in

the fact that the graduation address itself was given by Frederic Fleming, then the rector of Trinity Parish, which has sometimes been pictured as among the great real estate companies and is situated symbolically at the head of Wall Street. Back in 1927 he had been the tenth rector of St. Stephen's Church in Providence, Rhode Island. In 1946, I was to become the twelfth, but what God had in store for me as I graduated was something quite different.

Dr. Fleming had observed in his speech to the graduates that the state of the world we faced was like that of an uncontrolled flywheel on an enormous machine that was about to explode. I was not at all clear about the exact meaning of that strange figure of speech. Nor could I apply it to my first assignment. Having been ordained a deacon before my graduation, I was sent by Bishop Washburn to the very quiet suburban town of Maywood to serve a sort of internship at a little mission church dedicated to St. Martin. I found little evidence in Maywood of uncontrolled flywheels on an explosive world machine. But I knew that six months later, I would be raised to the Anglican priesthood and be appointed Vicar of Maywood on an annual salary of $1200, which certainly put off any wedding for awhile.

FOUR

A Good Man
Nowadays

Becoming the Vicar of Maywood sounded a bit like becoming a character in an eighteenth century novel. But Maywood, which was close to Hackensack, was truly suburban New Jersey and thus far removed from the quaint charms of the eighteenth century. There was, for example, no country squire with his family crest on his special pew, but there was one family which claimed certain proprietary rights over the little mission church because one of its members had contributed more than anyone else to the original building fund.

Although it was dedicated to St. Martin, the church itself did not in any way suggest the time and place in which he lived during the twilight of the Roman Empire. It was pure American suburban imitation of the California mission style, which was the sort of thing one used to see scattered in suburbia in the late twenties. Inspired by Hollywood, it might have been used on the set of a cowboy movie and an actor dressed as a kindly Franciscan friar would not have seemed out of place at the entrance. Certainly, it was not intended as the setting for an Anglican vicar in an eighteenth century novel.

The interior was bright but totally undistinguished and there was little adornment other than a plain brass cross flanked by two brass candlesticks on a plain wooden altar, which stood against the wall at the end of a little chancel, the aisle of which was between the choir stalls. In other words, the only thing Anglo-Catholic about the place was its new vicar, for the small congregation certainly thought of itself as respectably Protestant and had been very satisfied with the part-time services of the Low Church rector of a parish in a neighboring town, who had not done anything to alter this idea.

I found all this to be somewhat depressing, but as a lowly new deacon, there was little I could do to change things. Deacons were permitted to conduct the services of Morning and Evening Prayer, preach, baptize, conduct funerals, and perform other duties. But they could not celebrate the Eucharist or have any real administrative authority. And they had really nothing to say about the spiritual tone of the church community. They were two or three steps down the ladder from hospital interns in their first year.

The Eucharist was celebrated once a month by Canon William O. Leslie, who supervised such mission churches, which were not yet self-supporting, in various parts of the Diocese of Newark. Fortunately, Canon Leslie also administered the fiscal affairs of the mission, for that was precisely the sort of thing for which I had not been prepared by reading *The Parson's Handbook*.

I think that the high point of the time I served as a deacon at St. Martin's was the Christmas Eve of 1940, for Bishop Washburn himself came to celebrate the Eucharist in that rather obscure corner of his diocese, a gracious act that was typical of his truly pastoral attitude. Moreover, in this way he gave real support to my fledgling ministry.

I needed such support, as I am sure the bishop knew, for I

found Maywood to be a lonely outpost. There was, of course, no rectory; I rented a furnished room and took my meals some of the time with a very motherly Swedish landlady. Since marriage was now quite out of the question on my $1200 dollars a year, my long engagement was wisely ended by the young woman from Barnard. She had rightly given me up as a hopeless case, and I was now to have a bit of a taste of the loneliness that goes with the celibate life.

My six months as a deacon finally ended when I was ordained as a priest of the Episcopal Church by Bishop Washburn on February 1, 1941. This had been preceded by an ordination retreat at Holy Cross monastery, where I received final, practical instruction in the manner of celebrating the Eucharist in the proper Anglo-Catholic style, which was really the Roman Catholic style, as it was then set forth in Fortescue's *The Ceremonies of The Roman Rite Described.*

I was presented to the bishop for ordination by the retired rector of my boyhood parish, George P. Armstrong. As he had been a bit astonished when I first told him that I wished to enter the ministry, he seemed equally so to see that I had really done it.

The sermon at the ordination ceremony was preached by Norman Pittenger, whom I had come to know as a faculty member at the General Theological Seminary, where I had enrolled in a graduate program for the degree of Master of Sacred Theology. I went to classes at the Seminary once a week on my "day off" and experienced a happy escape from Maywood. Pittenger had an acquired British accent and a pleasantly liberal way of expressing traditional ideas in such a way as to avoid offending Protestant sensibilities. I had especially invited him to preach at my ordination because it was held at St. Martin's and I felt that he might manage to say something Catholic about the priesthood without seeming to be doing anything of the sort.

I was not disappointed, for while the congregation did not grasp all the implications of the preacher's learned remarks, they were all charmed by his style. Moreover, there was not so much as a murmur of disapproval when Bishop Washburn, in response to my request, invested me with the priestly vestments used at the Eucharist. Such things as chasubles had not previously appeared at St. Martin's, and they were not among the bishop's favorite garments, but once again he showed kindness to me by doing what I had asked and virtually giving his episcopal approval to the introduction of an Anglo-Catholic practice in a place where it had been previously unknown. I do not know how much discomfort this may have caused him, but I think it was not great. He was, after all, a bishop in the Episcopal Church and he had to have the ability to shift into high gear sometimes.

My mother, of course, believed that I was now on the way to becoming an Episcopal bishop myself, and the people of St. Martin's, most of whom came to receive my blessing, seemed genuinely happy for me. A great lot of cards and greetings poured in, some of which came from friends of my Columbia days.

There was one of these that touched my emotions more deeply than any of the others. It was from Father George Ford, who wrote me a warm letter, in which he said that had he not had to officiate at a wedding in his own parish near Columbia, he would certainly have been present at my ordination as a member of the congregation. He was not a man to make polite excuses. I believed what he wrote and I cried when I read it, for there was a moment when I would have given anything if my ordination could have taken place in St. Patrick's cathedral. Somewhere, deep down, I did know that although the ritual of ordination according to *The Book of Common Prayer* of the Episcopal Church employed the word *priest*, the Reformers who devised the rite originally had clearly intended to reject the Sacrifice of the Mass, which gave the priesthood its functional identity. Their intention was to ordain men to commemorate the Last Supper as ministers of a sacrament in which Christ might be present, but only to the faith of the believer.

However, putting aside such misgivings, as I was to do on many other occasions, I went on with my mission at St. Martin's and continued my graduate work at the seminary once a week. I was in the process of a reading course with Marshall Stewart, a fine theologian, in the *Summa Contra Gentiles* of Thomas Aquinas, whose thought had interested me ever since I first read Maritain in college. In fact, at Berkeley my sympathetic professor in systematic theology had encouraged me to study Aquinas and had guided me in the preparation of several extensive papers on Thomistic themes.

But such studies could not now occupy most of my time, for I was kept busy with pastoral duties and the round of hospital visits, census-taking, meetings with organizations, and developing a program of religious education for the children of St. Martin's. They at least, I hoped, might grow up to be good Anglo-Catholics. With the coming of Lent, there was also participation in the services of that season in other Episcopal churches in the area.

The very existence of one of these parishes and its Italian rector speaks volumes about the juxtaposition of opposites that is so characteristic of the Episcopal Church. This was the Episcopal Church of St. Anthony of Padua in Hackensack, which was situated in the very shadow of a large Irish Roman Catholic parish. Any lack of adornment in St. Martin's was more than made up for by the blatantly garish interior of St. Anthony's, with its hundreds of vigil candles, brightly colored statues, and a many-storied, soaring reredos behind the altar, which was equipped with six enormous candles, an overwhelming crucifix, and a ponderous tabernacle that faced out upon a spacious sanctuary that was adorned with hanging lamps. On a side altar stood a very large statue of St. Anthony of Padua, which was carried through the streets on his feast day to the sound of a brass band. This was hardly the atmosphere in which proper Episcopalians were accustomed to worship their God.

The rector was as exotic among Anglicans as was his church. Joe Anastasi had been born in Italy, where, it was said, he had received ordination as a deacon in the Roman Catholic Church. How or why he had come to the United States, I never knew. Nor did I ask him how or why he had come to be ordained as an Episcopalian priest. Certainly it had nothing to do with the option to marry, for he remained unmarried. That he continued to honor the Catholic Church was evident from the fact that in his sacristy there was a large picture of Pope Pius XI, which gazed across the room at a somewhat smaller picture of the Episcopalian bishop by whom Joe had been ordained.

At St. Anthony's the liturgy was not so much Anglo-Catholic as it was Anglo-Italian. During the Eucharist, various languages were used: Latin, much Italian, and heavily accented versions of the English of *The Book of Common Prayer*. The music on Sundays at High Mass or during the celebration of the patronal feast day was highly dramatic in the style of Italian opera. There were, for example, extended Glorias and Credos, during which the rector and any assisting deacons or subdeacons sat to one side in their vestments of Renaissance cut and raised their birettas at the mention of the Holy Name of Jesus, while the music soared upwards like fountains of liturgical scented water.

Whenever Joe Anastasi needed additional clergy for some big liturgical function, such as the Solemn High Mass of St. Anthony's Day, he would call for help among his Anglo-

Catholic circle of clerical friends—of whom I quickly became one—and they always were happy to be invited, not only because they enjoyed the somewhat eclectic but very Latin style of the liturgy but also because Joe was a wonderful host whose Italian dinners were unrivaled.

His unique presence among the clergy of the Episcopal Diocese of Newark was never more evident than it was on one memorable occasion at a clergy conference called to discuss one of the perennial proposals for the union of the Presbyterian and Episcopalian churches in the United States. To many in both of these churches such a union seemed logical. After all, their members moved in the same respectable social circles; quite a few belonged to the same country clubs; they represented jointly much of the New York Stock Exchange and were acknowledged leaders of the best in Anglo-Saxon Protestantism.

Bishop Washburn was pleased to introduce as the main speaker at the Episcopal Clergy Conference none other than Dr. Henry Sloane Coffin, the elegantly polished President of the Union Theological Seminary. Dr. Coffin had been pastor of New York's socially prestigious Madison Avenue Presbyterian Church and was a prominent figure in the General Assembly of the Presbyterian Church in the United States, of which he later became Moderator.

At the conclusion of Dr. Coffin's discourse about the many similarities which he thought existed between Episcopalians and Presbyterians, the distinguished speaker asked if there might be any questions. Up popped Joe Anastasi, whose accent clearly took Dr. Coffin by surprise.

Joe's question was put this way: "Dr. Coffin, if you gotta some of da bread and da wine left, after you are done with what you calla da Lord's Supper, what do you do with it?"

Dr. Coffin frowned thoughtfully for a moment before he replied, with some cautious hesitation, "Well, Sir, what we would probably do in such a case would be to pour the juice of the grape back into its flagon so that it would not be wasted. As for the bread, well, I don't know, but it might be thrown out on the lawn for the birds." Then in a burst of ecumenical inspiration, Dr. Coffin smiled and said, "Yes, that's it. We would give it to the birds, just like St. Francis."

Joe Anastasi looked thunderstruck and declared with some vehemence, "Dr. Coffin, let me tella you one thing for sure. Santo Francisco, he's never do that with the Blessed Sacrament."

The whole audience broke into loud laughter; there were no more questions. There was really no need. Joe had said it all. The meeting broke up for a delicious proper lunch, which Dr. Coffin seemed to enjoy, although he appeared to be looking around anxiously from time to time. Perhaps, he was looking for the presence of more strange characters in what he had supposed would be a gathering of familiar respectable ministers of the Protestant Episcopal Church in the United States of America. I suspect he might even have begun to wonder whether or not there would ever be a wedding with the Episcopalians, who seemed to have some very odd members in their family. To the best of my knowledge such a wedding has not yet taken place.

Much as my occasional association with St. Anthony's parish helped to brighten my otherwise colorless days in Maywood, I knew that I needed to leave St. Martin's for the very simple reason that I did not know enough about how to do the job of building a little mission into a parish. What I needed was to serve under an experienced parish priest who could teach me what my seminary studies had not. The only related training I had had was one summer spent as a seminarian working as a trainee in social case work at the Episcopal City Mission on Bleeker Street, just on the edge of Greenwich Village, which was a very long way from the world of middle class suburbia in Maywood.

I made my feelings known to Bishop Washburn, who just

happened to be looking for someone to fill the position of curate at Grace Church in Newark. The parish there had a very solid High Church tradition, as such things were commonly described, but it was not what the bishop thought of as an "extreme" Anglo-Catholic place and kept loyally to *The Book of Common Prayer*. He had heard of my excursions to St. Anthony's and was no doubt of the opinion that I would never grow up into a sensible churchman in that exotic environment, where Popes and Protestant bishops looked at each other across the sacristy. Consequently, I soon moved to Grace Church and had my first Sunday there on Pentecost, 1941. The music was magnificent; there was a well-trained boys choir; the vestments were richly red for the feast; there was even a modest amount of incense; and the liturgy was dignified. It was all very sensible, unlike St. Anthony's, with its wild street fiestas, its fireworks, its small brass cannon that boomed on the church steps at the Consecration of the Mass on festival days.

The rector of Grace Church, Charles Lewis Gomph, was most unlike other Episcopalian clergy I knew beause he was very German both in name and in appearance. In his Roman house cassock, which he always wore when on duty at the church office, he looked for all the world like the pastor of a town in the Bavarian Alps. His manner was friendly but always somewhat formal. In the two years I worked under him, he invariably addressed me by the title Father and almost never by my first name, even though a warm bond of affection developed and we seemed at times to be almost in a father-son relationship.

He lived with two unmarried sisters in a rectory in what was then a fine residential part of Newark, quite far removed from the church, which was downtown on Broad Street, just in front of the main post office. When he said a weekday Mass, he always had his very austere breakfast in his study in the parish office which was located in a large building attached to the church. This frugal meal, like his equally frugal lunch, was served by one of three nuns of the Sisters of St. Margaret, whose convent was on the top floor of the building and who ran the religious education program and did other work in the parish as well. This group of nuns came from their motherhouse, situated on Lewisburg Square in Boston, and were part of what was then a fine and flourishing religious community in the Episcopal Church. I do not recall ever having visited the sisters in their residence, which was reached by elevator and had what was virtually a cloistered status.

From the outset, the rector had made it clear that the tradition of the parish was that its clergy were unmarried. I was at that point happy to be part of such a tradition and delighted by the precise way in which the rector scheduled my time and laid out my duties. In addition to early daily Masses, I would have my share of evening devotions, funerals, baptisms, and weddings. I was to have a men's Bible class, give instructions in my turn at the Sunday Family Mass, and do most of the parish census work. In addition, I was put in charge of the youth organization and given charge of training the altar boys. I was to have my share of sick calls, hospital visits, and a regular list of shut-ins who received Holy Communion at home once each month. On Saturday afternoons and evenings, I was to hear confessions, for this was a parish where the Sacrament of Penance was administered, which was, of course, not the case in places that were not of the High Church or Anglo-Catholic variety. At Berkeley those who were so disposed were given an opportunity to study classical Catholic and Anglican moral theology and to be examined as to their knowledge of it. Consequently, I had not only had the experience of having myself been going to confession regularly for many years but I was also conversant with the appropriate theology of the sacrament.

I lived at first in a room at the Newark Athletic Club, for there were no quarters for the curate at the church. Shortly, however, I rented a pleasant apartment which I shared with my mother, who had retired from teaching. I felt that at last my life had taken a firm, constructive direction. Indeed, it seemed that I might even be on the way to becoming the sort of sensible churchman that Bishop Washburn hoped I would be.

For one thing, my concerns with the politics of social change, which had played so large a part in my Columbia career, had undergone major changes. Long ago the reality of the Soviets under Stalin had exposed the complete naivete of people who, like myself, had once believed that Communism and Christianity could be reconciled. The purges and terror, the 1939 Soviet-Nazi pact, and the brutal partition of Poland taught lessons that seem to have been totally forgotten by proponents of so-called liberation theology in parts of Latin America and elsewhere.

Moreover, much of the Marxian dogma about the polarization of wealth in the modern industrial nations had been shattered in Britain and America, where whole segments of the industrial work force joined the middle class and trades unions became powerful corporate interests. And there was certainly no evidence in Soviet Russia that the State was about to wither away, as the Marxists had claimed that it would eventually do. Instead a new elite had arisen and Stalin made the power of czars of the past as nothing beside that of his totalitarian dictatorship, equipped as it was with weapons created by modern technology that could easily crush any and all political opposition in Russia.

Even Roosevelt's New Deal appeared to be working because the war which had broken out in Europe in 1939 had accelerated the whole American economy and real domestic

problems were only apparently being solved by war production to provide weapons and supplies for the Allies. When in
1940 Roosevelt had won election for a third term, he had
even promised that America would not become involved in
the fighting but would continue to prosper by becoming the
"arsenal of democracy."

Now it was the war that was the political issue, as we all
debated the question of our own possible involvement.
Thus, although I thought that my life had now taken a firm
direction in my work at Grace Church under the guidance of
Father Gomph, I was also very much aware that it could be
suddenly redirected. How much longer, I wondered, could
we keep out of the war against Hitler? And if we did become
involved, what would that mean for me?

The desperate Battle of Britain had already involved some
Americans in combat since, like one young man from our
parish, a number had gone to join the R.A.F. in Canada.
Hitler had attacked the Russians in the very month that I had
come to Grace Church and by the end of the year both
Moscow and Leningrad were under seige, the Red Army
was everywhere in retreat and the Germans were in the
Crimea. At home Americans debated whether or not we
should enter the conflict or allow the two totalitarian nations to destroy one another. But what would this mean for
our place in the world, especially if Britain could no longer
carry on its lonely battle in the West?

For me the answer to some of these questions came just as
I was holding a meeting with some parish young people to
plan for a Christmas party and dance. It was the afternoon of
Sunday, December 7, 1941. Pearl Harbor had been bombed
with great losses and we were in the world conflict. I felt, as I
said to a congregation gathered in the church for Evening
Prayer that night, as if the walls of our whole world were on
fire.

At first, however, the life of the parish went on more or

less as usual, except for the young, whose plans were now quite uncertain and the pace of their lives accelerated. Yet together we planned excursions and parties and I took some of the young men of draft age on a retreat at Holy Cross Monastery. More and more new jobs meanwhile began to open up for young women, some of which were in types of industrial production in which women had not been previously employed. We began to hear of a character called "Rosie the Riveter." That summer of 1942 it seemed that somehow the number of funerals in the parish was greatly increasing; the rector was on vacation, and I was constantly burying the dead. There seemed to be a portent in this, for one became increasingly aware that Newark and Grace Church would be very different places in the future.

Gasoline rationing, previously unknown in America, made me all the more aware of how much the parish no longer resembled what it must have been when its people lived nearby. Calling on parishoners in the census work meant doing a great deal of driving. Not a few families were as much as forty-five minutes or an hour away out in the suburbs. Indeed, there were actually people registered as members of the parish and active contributors who lived outside the United States and received the parish bulletin regularly.

It had been in the course of visiting the parishoners in November, 1941 that the rector asked me to look in on a family named Cole. This family lived in the town of Irvington and had a son who had left his studies at Columbia to join the R.A.F., where his life was, of course, in daily peril. On the occasion of my visit I met both Mrs. Cole and her mother, a delightful old German woman who had been raised as a Catholic but who attended Grace Church. They told me that another member of the family, a young girl, was also at home but that if I wished to meet her, I would have to go outside to a pigeon coop in the backyard, for she was out there feeding her father's racing pigeons, as she did after coming home from high school.

This youngest member of the household, who was fifteen, was named Mildred. She was, in fact, the only member of the family who came to church without fail every Sunday. When I opened the door of the pigeon coop there was a noisy cloudburst of pigeon feathers, dust, and birdseed, as the pigeons reacted to my entrance. In the midst of this cloud appeared Mildred Cole, a very attractive but very embarrassed young girl, whom I had seen at church but never met. Her sixteenth birthday was to be in the following month but, in spite of her evident confusion caused by my unexpected entrance, she seemed more mature than she was, and I sensed in her something unusual, something of the look I have been privileged to see a very few times in my life. I did not know quite what it was then, but I have come to recognize it when I encounter it. I am speaking of a quality of character that shines in the eyes of people whose faith runs deep, far deeper than my own. After a few moments of polite parochial conversation I left.

But I found the experience disturbing because I was attracted to her as if she were a woman five or six years older than she actually was, and I had determined that I was not going to become emotionally involved with any woman, whatever her age. It seemed clear to me that being a priest is really not a profession like medicine or law. Being a priest means serving not only one's fellow human beings as a representative of the Church but also it means giving one's whole being over to a special relationship with Christ that should involve all one's love. Or so I had come to believe. Thus I felt that any woman who was married to a priest would surely sometimes find herself in the unenviable position of seeming to compete with God. And that is a very different thing from having to compete with a job or a secretary or some other woman in her husband's life.

I had, it was true, met and occasionally dated a woman whom I had known in high school and who was a nurse in one of the hospitals I visited regularly. We had had a good many happy times together, but when she had showed a serious interest in our becoming married, I more or less convinced her that this would not be in her best interest. I was most relieved when she finally married an Irish Roman Catholic policeman.

Things did not turn out quite that way with Mildred Cole. In spite of some misgivings on my part, when I met her at church or in the young people's meetings I at first began talking to her as if she were just a nice kid with an interest in her school work, her music, and her religion. But then I became more and more attracted to her both physically and as a person who seemed strangely wise beyond her years, with a somewhat sad kind of wisdom and a great longing after the kind of happiness that this world really cannot give. Thus it was that our relationship finally reached the point at which I felt it necessary to explain to her—even as I had explained to my friend from high school days—that marriage to me would be nothing but a disaster for her. As things finally turned out sometime later, she did not find this to be at all convincing.

Meanwhile, I paid a visit to Father Damasus Winzen, who had been one of the Benedictines I had known at Berkeley. At that time he was teaching at the seminary of the Newark Archdiocese at Darlington. There I was much impressed by what was in those days before Vatican II like many other such flourishing seminaries in the United States, with a large contingent of young men in cassocks who appeared to me to be at once both happy, well-adjusted, and disciplined. If they were not, they were certainly putting on a good show. Later I also visited Father Damasus in Keyport, after a temporary spot had been found for some of the monks to live in the United States.

There we talked of Dean Ladd after his death, which took place in 1941. Father Damasus had written to Mrs. Ladd, "I know how deeply he understood and loved the Eucharist." I agreed and commented that the Dean's Church History course had made me see how it was that the papacy had inevitably become the center of unity for the mainstream of Christianity. I said that I often wondered where I really was in relation to that mainstream and its obvious historic center. And Damasus looked at me most kindly, as he said, "Someday we will be one again."

Pursuing my studies in Thomism in my graduate course, which I continued to follow at the General Theological Seminary, I sometimes had occasion to visit the library of St. Mary's Abbey on High Street, where I became acquainted with the librarian, Father Irenaeus, and was presented to the Abbot, Patrick O'Brien.

Through those associations, I also met some Benedictine nuns, whom I visited at their convent in Maplewood. With them, as in other contacts I had with Catholic religious and diocesan clergy, I felt a common bond which I did not have with many Episcopalian clergy outside the small Anglo-Catholic circle. It was truly a source of the greatest sadness to realize that we who called ourselves Anglo-Catholics were separated from our Roman Catholic brethren by an ancient accident of dismal politics.

Thus there were certain times of depression in my life when I wondered whether or not I should have become a Roman Catholic in the days when I had almost done so at Columbia. But the image and example of Charles Gomph was there to show me that what certainly looked like the life of an exemplary priest, who embodied a truly Catholic faith, could somehow be lived in the Episcopal Church.

As a matter of fact, my work as a curate was outwardly

progressing so well that the rector spoke of the possibility that someday I might succeed him. My youth work centered more and more around an organization associated with the Holy Cross Monastery and called The Servants of Christ the King. There were a number of branches in the metropolitan area and our Grace Church branch was always in the forefront of the spiritual and social action programs. In April 1942, Grace Church was the host for a big rally and morale was very high. Moreover, I was appointed to the diocesan Board of Religious Education and published an article on that subject in *Action*, a publication of the New York diocese that was edited by Anglo-Catholics.

I was also advancing towards my graduate degree at the General Theological Seminary and preparing my thesis beneath a statue of Thomas Aquinas in my little study at the parish office.

My topic had to do with St. Thomas' concept of personality. It was heavily influenced by such Roman Catholic luminaries of that era as Jacques Maritain, Romono Guardini, Etienne Gilson, Anton Pegis, and Dietrich von Hildebrand.

Thomism was not exactly the cup of tea of the General Theological Seminary. I remember that when I was making my formal defense before the faculty, the Dean, who was an Old Testament type sometimes likened to Jeremiah, seemed to be asleep. At the end of the questions and my responses, however, he shook himself in his academic gown, rather like a giant condor rousing itself for predatory flight, and looked balefully at me in silence. Finally he said, "Where, amid all this scholastic abstraction, does one find the Great Sinai God?" I replied, somewhat archly, "Mr. Dean, he is present disguised as Pure Actuality." The Dean then shook himself again and returned to his somnolence. In any case I did receive my degree.

Shortly thereafter, Bishop Washburn appointed me as an

Examining Chaplain. In those days a board of clergy bearing that title used to examine diocesan candidates for ordination. The candidates had to pass these examinations before the bishop could proceed to ordain them.

I served as an Examining Chaplain only once, for in February, 1943, with the very reluctant consent of my rector, I asked Bishop Washburn to permit me to apply for appointment as a Chaplain in the United States Navy, which was the only channel through which I could become a chaplain working with Marines. I felt that I had to share the war experience of my generation and be of some help to men in combat, which was certainly where one would be with the Marines.

The Bishop granted this request, with the very gracious comment that Father Gomph would certainly find it hard to be without me in the parish. I was most sincerely moved to be told that, for it meant that I really had done useful pastoral work and gained the approval of one of the few really good men I had ever known, for Charles Gomph was such a man in a terrible time of the world's growing darkness.

FIVE

The Navy Way

My decision to volunteer as a military chaplain in the winter of 1943 was probably caused, in part, by things other than a simple desire to share my generation's historical moment and be of service to Marines in combat. It may have also been a way of coping with my own inner conflicts about celibacy, as well as those caused by the attraction I felt for the Roman Catholic Church. Somewhere in the back of my mind there was the idea that going off to become a chaplain would at least put these problems "on the shelf" for the time being, while I was busy participating in the world conflict.

I was not, as I quickly discovered in my work with men in the military service, alone in this feeling of being able to put my civilian problems "on the shelf." There were indeed many who were not unhappy about leaving behind, for the time being, such things as creditors, domestic stresses, and boring jobs. I found that if American participation in World War II was in any sense to be thought of as a crusade, the crusaders were not unlike those of the medieval time, who may safely be said to have had all sorts of mixed motives for going off to fight Saracens. Some of them, it will be recalled, were not above sacking the Christian city of Constantinople on their way to liberate Jerusalem.

Of course Americans felt that we were in the war because

we had been attacked. The Japanese had made it impossible for the isolationists to argue their case any longer, and the Nazis had, in support of their ally, declared war on us three days after the attack on Pearl Harbor. It was a popular war with the general public, unlike the later tragic conflict in Vietnam.

If there was not quite the same naive patriotic fervor that had swept the country in World War I, there was nonetheless a lot of the same kind of political rhetoric, at least on the ward level. Before entering the Navy, for example, I recall an occasion when I sat on a platform out of doors, having given the invocation at a ceremony honoring the men of one of Newark's political wards who had been, as it was said, "called to serve the colors." Beside me sat a Catholic priest, who was waiting to give a benediction at the end of the ceremony. One of his parishoners, who was Commissioner of Public Safety, was giving the main address to an audience largely made up of female relatives of the men being honored.

This orator was of the white-maned, florid, silver-tongued variety commonly heard from on civic occasions. Reaching the climax of his speech and perspiring from the effort he had made, this gentleman declared, "You in this fine audience who are mothers, you are well acquainted with pain and suffering. And I want you all to know that I know what it means to be the mother of a soldier."

There wasn't a dry eye in the hushed audience, but as we walked off the platform at the end of the ceremony, my Roman Catholic opposite number gently put his arm around the orator's broad shoulder and said, "John, you must be the only man in Newark who knows what it is to be a mother."

Such bombast was happily absent from the announcement that I was about to become a military chaplain. Father

Gomph wrote a simple statement for the Parish Bulletin and observed that all were aware of what he called my "unusual fitness for the work of a Chaplain in the Armed Forces." He went on to say that for this reason the parish was happy "to lend Father Thomson to the Government for the duration."

The "unusual fitness" for military service I was described as having was the rector's reference to the time I had spent in the Platoon Leaders training program at Quantico during my Columbia days. I am not at all sure that this six weeks of training by experts in combat made me especially fit to be a chaplain, but I do know that the indoctrination given to me by my Marine mentors certainly worked. As I told the rector, I was just not interested in being a chaplain with any but a Marine Corps unit, for there were, I said, none better. I shared the notion of the Marines that the Army, Navy, and Air Force were supporting "allies" of America's real fighting force, the United States Marine Corps. And I must confess that more than forty years later I really haven't changed my mind.

I had, of course, been distressed when I had learned that in order to have even the chance of becoming a chaplain with Marines, I would have to be accepted by the Navy. Every Marine was a fighting man, I was told, and the Corps had to get its doctors, medical corpsmen, and chaplains from the Navy. I do not recall that any mention was made of the fact that there were some Marines who were not even potentially fighting men because they were, in fact, women. At that time it appeared that these female Marines were thought of by old timers in the Corps as members of a sort of Women's Auxiliary that had been forced on the Marines by Eleanor Roosevelt, who secretly wanted to join the Raiders and lead an assault on Japan.

After what seemed too long a time, I was accepted by the Navy and the Army and Navy Commission of the Episcopal Church, which certified Episcopal priests for military chaplaincies. I purchased the appropriate uniforms and was scheduled to depart for the Navy's School for Chaplains, which was then situated on the campus of William and Mary College in Williamsburg, Virginia.

I had completed my S.T.M. work at the General Theological Seminary, despite the Dean's distaste for scholasticism, but I would have to receive the degree by mail since the formal commencement was to be on May 26 and I was scheduled to depart for Williamsburg on May 14.

During the time when I had been finishing my thesis in my study at the church, I had had, as I have mentioned, a statue of St. Thomas Aquinas on a shelf gazing down at me as I wrote about his ideas of personality. An assistant sexton, who was an Irish Roman Catholic from a Dominican parish, always dusted this statue with great care and reverence. His farewell words to me were, "Father, I'll take the saint home with me where he'll be more comfortable. I'll look after him and I know he'll be looking after you."

The senior sexton, a very elderly German named Michael, also assured me of his prayers and that I would be remembered when he went to Mass at St. Mary's Abbey where he was the oldest active parishoner. He knew of my friendship with some of the Benedictines and always treated me as if he and I had a mutual secret between us. One evening, for example, not long before I left for the Navy, Michael and I were out in the sacristy after a service at which the rector had preached a sermon in which he had said that St. Peter had never been given authority over the other Apostles. Michael had been listening, and as the rector came into the sacristy, the old man said to him, "Ja, ja, Father Gomph, maybe it's right what you say, I don't know. Only one thing I know, which is that Peter is still Peter." Before anything else could be said, Michael winked at me and quickly disappeared out the sacristy door.

Thus I knew that whatever else I might have had going for

me as a chaplain approved by the Navy and the Protestant Episcopal Church, I certainly did have the prayers of not one but two Catholic sextons, which for all I know, may have helped to account for the fact that I survived the war.

I did not lack for prayers and good wishes from the people of the parish. The annual Parish Dinner was held on May 12 and was planned most generously as my going-away party. The dining room was jammed with people, all of whom loudly applauded an announcement that I would return to Grace Church after the war. I was given a money gift, to which parishoners of all ages and conditions had contributed to show their affection. My mother was given an orchid corsage, and the parish bulletin, in describing the event said that her "brave and cheerful spirit was admired by all."

For the moment I had become a local celebrity, even to the point of being asked to sign autographs on pictures that had been made of me in my new uniform. This was, I know, by no means a unique experience, for thousands of us who went off to World War II received abundant signs of appreciation and support from those we left at home. And our return was also hailed when it was over. That was the kind of experience which has wrongfully not been given to those who have served this country well in combat in such places as Korea and Vietnam.

When I entered the doors of the Chaplains School in Williamsburg, I entered what was to be for the next eight weeks a sort of Never-Never-Land, where the floor became a deck; the ceiling an overhead; the walls bulkheads; and a visiting admiral was "piped aboard" what was not a ship but a campus building, while chaplains fresh from civilian altars and pulpits stood at attention and "lined the rails."

Indeed, the arrival of the admiral, which took place near the end of our training, involved so much parading and preparatory drilling that Father Frank Sullivan, S.J.—back from overseas and on the so-called faculty—said to some of us confidentially, "Boys, the administration of this school really thinks that the arrival of this admiral is at least as important as the Second Coming of Christ."

The administration to which he referred was made up of a few Regular Navy Chaplains, as distinguished from us who were classified as mere Reserves. The Commanding Officer, as he was called, was a Baptist preacher who had made the Naval Chaplaincy his career. That he took himself and the Navy very seriously may be seen from the manner in which he greeted each new chaplain at his introductory interview. Seated most solemnly behind a great desk and flanked by the flags of the United States and the Navy Department, he would intone the following question: "Chaplain, just what was your religion before you joined the Navy?" The implication was clearly that whatever one's religion had been, it was now somehow superseded by membership in the Navy.

In the Navy's view of the world it ruled on land or sea, there were three varieties of chaplains, in the following order: Protestants, Catholics, and Jews, to correspond to the recognized pluralism of American religious life. A chaplain who was not a Jewish rabbi or a Catholic priest, was simply a Protestant until a concession was finally made for the Orthodox. The enormous variety of American Protestant sects and divisions was such that even the Navy bureaucracy could not keep track of it.

Each Saturday morning when I was at Wllliamsburg there was a strange, if not bizarre, "worship service" that was billed as the "General Protestant Communion Service." I never attended this remarkable event, but I learned of it from a couple of chaplains who belonged to the Lutheran Missouri Synod and went to it just once, perhaps out of morbid curiosity. They reported that the ceremonies were so ecumenical that the one rabbi in our class, who was clearly very, very "reformed," had actually received some of the bread and grape juice that was served.

Somewhat bewildered by this, these Lutherans reported that they had questioned the Commanding Officer about it. His reply was this historic statement: "Chaplains, I hope you will now realize that what the churches have not accomplished in two thousand years, the United States Navy has done in six weeks."

Whatever it was that the Chaplains School did by way of teaching and testing our class of forty-five assorted clergymen in preparing them for duty in the Navy could probably have been done in less than half the time, including the apprentice period each of us spent on a naval installation, where it was to be determined whether or not we would be able to "fit in" to the world of the Navy, which was certainly unlike any other.

Some of the instruction was nothing less than ludicrous. For example, the Regular Navy chaplain who headed the school and who had clearly always wanted to play the part of a line officer would begin a first class of the day by calling us to attention and saying, "Gentlemen, when I walk through that door to this classroom, no matter what the clock up there on the wall says, it is 0800 hours." The silly part of it was that he really meant it and expected to be taken seriously.

Perhaps the height of the instructional absurdity was attained by one of the faculty who taught a course called Corollary Duties, which included all sorts of jobs that might be given to a chaplain other than those associated with specifically religious activities or pastoral work. Speaking with a soft Southern accent, our instructor very slowly developed the thought that on some ships or naval shore stations we might possibly be placed in charge of the library.

"What," he asked with a thoughtful frown and a friendly

smile, "does a sailor expect to find when he goes into a Navy library?" Then after a significant pause, he answered his own question by saying, "Books, gentlemen, books."

When our class, known as Class 10–43, graduated on July 18, 1943, there were—true to the Navy categories— three class valedictorians: Protestant, Catholic, and the one rabbi in the class, who was easily chosen as the Jewish vale-dictorian. I was chosen, for reasons still mysterious to me, to be the Protestant valedictorian. I do not remember anything of what I said, but I have never forgotten the speech of the Catholic valedictorian, who was born in Ireland and spoke with a fine brogue. His speech, which I give in its perfect entirety, was wildly applauded when he finished saying: "I have come to the conclusion after eight weeks of careful de-liberation that the purpose of this institution is to bring the student from a state of total confusion to one of passive res-ignation." Perhaps, after all, there could not have been a better preparation for what was yet to come. Passive resigna-tion was a useful state of mind in the Navy.

There was, as the adage ran, a right way, a wrong way, and a Navy way of doing things. For example, I had some knowledge of the Marine Corps, had expressed a preference for duty with Marines, and was eager to be assigned to serve with Marine infantry. The Navy way was, however, to make use of me at the Naval Training Station at Bainbridge, Mary-land, where I had served my training apprenticeship and where there was not, as far as I could see, a Marine any-where in sight. Not only were there no Marines, there were very few Episcopalians, except for the top brass, all of whom were apparently not only graduates of the Naval Academy but Episcopalians as well. At first I was assigned as the Prot-estant Chaplain of a recruit regiment, which meant that I would be working with new recruits in the training gener-ally described as "boot camp." The great majority were from the rural South and their religious background was intensely evangelical. As one of the lads said to me, "Where I come from we don't think we've been to church unless the preacher climbs the tent pole." On Sundays I conducted the Episcopal service of Holy Communion, which Anglo-Catholics called Mass, at an early hour. Later, in a vast drill hall, I conducted a service of readings, hymns, preaching and prayer that was described as the General Protestant Service. Needless to say, I did not climb any poles but did my best to preach the Gospel. I hope some of them felt that they had been to church, but as they were all marched in and marched out I had no way of interviewing them on that or any other subject.

My Catholic counterpart in the recruit regiment was Father Bill Cooney, a priest of about my age, who came from Chicago. Our Senior Chaplain was a much older priest, Father Bill Martin, who came from Troy, New York and treated the two of us as he might have done if we had been his curates. Since he was a very kind man, this was a good thing from every point of view.

Our respective offices were almost adjacent in an area that also contained a library. Remembering the sage advice of our teacher at Chaplains School, I was pleased to note that there were a great many books available for any sailor who might come there for the purpose of reading, but there were not many who did so. They were too busy learning the Navy way of doing things and were therefore a group of very confused young men in the process of reaching the state of passive resignation which would make Navy life no less incomprehensible but at least endurable.

Bill Cooney's desk was nearer the main entrance than mine. Consequently, incoming recruits in search of a chaplain, or a book, would most frequently go to speak to him first. Most were youngsters from remote rural areas who sometimes gave the impression that in addition to being Protestants they were also not good at communicating with strangers, especially those that wore officer's uniforms. Bill, of course, took malicious delight in saying to those who were evidently a bit on the "dim" side, "I am sorry, but I think you must want to see the Protestant chaplain." One day, however, there was one such individual who turned out to be a Catholic—a recent convert from somewhere deep in the hills, who explained that he was having trouble remembering how to say the Our Father and the Hail Mary. Bill was a bit less cocksure after that.

Apart from conducting services, most of our work was with recruits who had personal problems which, unless they had to do with marriages, usually had little or nothing to to with religion.

Some days we did very little, which was something that was not limited to chaplains, for as someone has said, "War is long periods of boredom interspersed by moments of great excitement."

A case in point which may illustrate some of the way I spent my time is that of a young recruit who appeared at my desk looking especially awkward in his dungaree uniform because it did not quite fit his very tall, very thin, very angular figure. His head, disfigured as it was by the barbaric recruit haircut, hung dejectedly and his big jaw was slack, as he mumbled, "Chaplain, I got misery."

A series of questions finally revealed the source of his "misery" when he said, "My daddy has a horse farm and I grew up with horses. I likes horses better than I likes most people, and since I've been in this here Navy, I just ain't seen no horses at all."

Showing my own dreadful ignorance of the Army, I politely asked why he had not joined the cavalry. He then explained that the cavalry used means of transport other than horses but a recruiter had told him that the Navy had a mounted beach patrol which was always on the lookout for German submarines. What he wanted me to do was to find out if he could be assigned to such a beach patrol when he got out of his recruit training.

On that occasion I think I was inspired, for I suddenly recalled hearing that there was a mounted Shore Patrol unit that rode around the perimeter of the Training Station to discourage those who might wish to leave without proper authorization. Aided by the good offices of the Shore Patrol people, I actually managed to solve this unusual case. In fact the last thing I saw when I left Bainbridge was this same fellow out near the main gate, mounted on a horse and preparing to make his rounds somewhat incongruously dressed in Navy dungarees with his little white cap set squarely on his cropped head. He looked very happy.

After awhile I was moved from the recruit work and made what was called the Ship's Company Chaplain, which meant that I was to serve the staff of the Training Station itself. I had the special responsibility of conducting the Protestant services in the main Chapel, where the Commanding Officer, the Executive Officer, and their wives always graced the principal Protestant Sunday morning service with their presence. They were nice people with pleasant manners who enjoyed good music played on a good organ as an embellishment to a formal worship service that closely resembled the style of *The Book of Common Prayer*, to which they were accustomed.

I took over this new post from the glamorous Chaplain Donald Aldrich, who had been rector of the very liberal Broad Church Episcopalian parish called the Church of the Ascension, which was one of the more fashionable New York churches. A strikingly handsome, tall man with very carefully groomed iron-grey hair, Donald Aldrich was known as a pulpit performer of great personal magnetism, who was very good at making people feel very good. Before leaving Bainbridge, he confided to me that whenever he celebrated Holy Communion during warm weather, he never read the Gospels prescribed because they were "too full of myths and miracles." He preferred, he said, selections from Emerson or from his own works, which had more modern popular appeal. He advised me to do the same because the Commanding Officer liked it that way.

Needless to say, my Anglo-Catholic sensibilities were such that I did not take his advice. When I celebrated the Episcopal Communion Service, I read the assigned Gospel, even in the august presence of the Commanding Officer, who did not seem to notice any difference; nor did he appear to be in any way disturbed by my chasuble, which was obviously different from Chaplain Aldrich's customary surplice and stole. There was, in fact, some reason to believe that he was actually not paying much attention.

After all, Saturday evenings often called for the expenditure of a lot of social energy by the officers of the Ship's Company and not everyone was always in top form on Sunday mornings. This was the old "Navy Way" and there were even those outside experts on military affairs who dared to claim that Saturday night sociability might possibly have had something to do with the apparent lack of alertness when the Japanese had chosen to attack Pearl Harbor on a Sunday morning.

As things developed, I naturally found "the Navy Way" to be very enjoyable. The food was excellent, the quarters were comfortable, and there was a fine golf course. I probably could have stayed at Bainbridge for the duration. There was no shortage of Protestant Navy chaplains and I was getting along very well with the formidable group of senior officers' wives who really controlled things at the main chapel and were known as "The Grey Ladies," not because of the color of their hair but because of the color of the outfits they wore when doing charitable good works.

One of the great attractions was the congeniality of my fellow officers of the staff of the Training Station. Many of these friendly fellows were dentists, whose job it was to examine the teeth of hundreds of incoming recruits. Their chief worry seemed to be whether or not they would be able to meet their assigned quotas of fillings each week. Thus there were many pleasant social gatherings, at one of which my guest was Mildred Cole, with whom I had been having some sporadic correspondence. She came down from Newark one weekend for a party and stayed with the family of one of our friendly dentists. Later in the war this same dental officer died when his ship was torpedoed in the Pacific. That, of course, was also part of the Navy, as it was called upon to do the real job for which it was intended. At Bainbridge, however, such things seemed very far away.

While I remained there, I learned that I was the envy of some of my priest friends from Class 10–43, one of whom had to suffer through the whole war as Chaplain of the Waves' main barracks in Washington, D.C. I was certainly comfortable, but I was not content. I had once been touched by Marine Corps madness, and it was with Marines that I wanted to be.

I finally got my chance in typical Navy style, which means that it came as the result of pure chance, some good luck, and a bit of influence. One weekend I had managed some time off to take part in an Episcopal church service at a socially prominent parish in Baltimore. At lunch afterwards I happened to meet a Navy Captain from the Bureau of Naval Personnel, the place where all our assignments were made. I told him of where I was stationed and of my desire to serve with Marines.

His reaction was that of any normal man. "Chaplain," he said, "You have to be either crazy or kidding." I admitted that the former might be the case, for I was not kidding. I went further and importuned him to help me to get a Marine assignment as soon as he could when he got back to his Washington desk. He shook his head in disbelief, but he said that he would do as I asked. He was a product of Annapolis, a Southerner, and a gentleman of his word. In less than ten days, I was ordered to take some leave and then to proceed to the big Marine Corps installation at Camp Pendleton in Oceanside, California.

After a brief time at home, I took my travel orders and went, as was usual in those days, by train to my destination on the West Coast. It was mid-December of 1943, and I was eager to change my blue Navy uniform for the sacred green of the Marine Corps.

SIX

Somebody Other
Than Ourselves

Arriving in Los Angeles enroute to Oceanside, I had the impression, perhaps derived from seeing many Hollywood films, that the whole sprawling place was really nothing but a movie set, which would be taken down anytime in the near future. And the more I saw of it, the more I felt that it might be rather a good thing if a vast fleet of trucks would indeed come some night and haul the whole place away.

When I finally reached Camp Pendleton, I entered upon one of those times, so common in military life, when one waits for days on end for orders to go somewhere else. As was almost always the case, there were too many Protestant chaplains and not enough Catholic ones around the vast stretches of Pendleton. I was sent, for example, to the Raider Battalion Training Center, which already had a very competent Protestant chaplain, but no Catholic chaplain to serve the majority of the men.

This was the first, but not the last, time I experienced the feeling of being superfluous. I had nothing that I could do for the Raider Battalion and there was apparently nothing they could do with me. Finally, I was given the "corollary duty" of running the Officers Club, which operated slot machines and was constantly in need of food, beer, and booze, especially that which took the form of a blended whiskey that was nicknamed "Schenley's Black Death."

That this responsibility did not disturb me at all may be taken as further evidence that I was really on the Catholic side. I suppose that nothing more marked the difference in moral theology between Catholic and Protestant chaplains than their general attitudes regarding two topics: "the Demon Rum" and artificial birth control. For example, a Jesuit friend who was a Catholic chaplain at Great Lakes Naval Training Station once told me that when he had complained to his Baptist Senior Chaplain about the sale of contraceptives in the Ship's Store, the gruff reply was, "I don't care about that, but I thank God that at least they don't sell beer."

We did not, to my knowledge, sell contraceptives at the Raiders' Officers Club and neither my colleague nor I had any problem with the sales of beer or, for that matter, other alcoholic beverages. My colleague, I should note, was a Lutheran of ample Germanic size.

As for the slot machines, I saw them, as well as other forms of gambling, as quite harmless; the serious business at the Training Center was learning how to gamble one's life in commando-type attacks on Japanese forces. I was happy enough to be of some use, but most of the time all I had to do was sign my name on an abundance of government requisition forms.

In any event, even that light duty ended when the Marine Corps decided to terminate the Raiders as a special force of elite assault troops on the perfectly logical ground that all Marines were elite assault troops. I might add that the closing days and nights of the Raider Battalion Training Center seemed to have their focal point at the club. I may not have had much work as a chaplain, but at least I was at the center of things.

After the last rites, so to speak, had been performed over the Raider Battalion, I lived at the big Bachelor Officers Quarters at Pendleton and waited for orders in a suspended state of boredom. My escape from it was my discovery, one lonely weekend, of the Episcopal Church of St. James in La Jolla, where I had been wandering about. The rector of the parish was an Englishman named Donald Glazebrook and I have never met a more kindly and hospitable man than he was. Indeed, he reminded me greatly of Father Gomph in his whole pastoral style. Yet he was married and had several offspring about. His devotion to his work was certainly exemplary, and he made me wonder if, after all, a married priest might not also be, like Father Gomph, totally committed to his vocation as a priest. His wife was a matronly person who appeared to share his vocation with him and went about doing a lot of good, but not the kind that is simply going about.

The parish was somewhere between being High Church and being Anglo-Catholic. In other words, in this respect it was much like Grace Church in Newark, but it had not gone quite that far. On Sundays there was always a Eucharist, announced as Holy Communion, at seven thirty in the morning. More often than not, the later service at eleven was that of Morning Prayer. In between there was the traditional Sunday School. Something of the flavor of the place may be gained from the way in which Donald Glazebrook announced hours for Confessions in his Sunday bulletin: "The Rector will be in the church from 7:00 to 7:30 P.M. on the Saturday before the first Sunday of the month." Only the truly initiated knew what this cryptic message meant.

I might have remained at Camp Pendleton until peace came, quite alone and evidently forgotten, had I not visited St. James and helped out with services there, for it was in that parish that I met the wife of a Marine Corps General and confided to her that beautiful as LaJolla was, I very much wanted to be assigned to a Marine unit overseas. Her husband commanded a whole division overseas and she promised to write to him about me.

I would not think of suggesting that assignments in the Marine Corps are in any way affected by the wives of generals, but not too long after I had talked with this lady in La Jolla, I received orders to report to the prestigious and battle-hardened First Marine Division, which—as I later learned—had been in action on the island of New Britain and was currently undergoing something euphemistically described as "resupply and training" at an island base called Pavuvu. This palmy paradise was in a group of islands called the Russells, located about a hundred miles north of the fabled Guadalcanal, where the Division had inflicted upon the Japanese their first major military setback in the Pacific war back in 1942–43.

The troop transport left San Diego on April 18, after I had been given fond farewells by the Glazebrooks and some of my new friends at St. James-by-the-Sea—to give the parish its full title. The voyage seemed endlessly slow. The feeling of many of us was, perhaps, best expressed by a young Marine I noticed one day gazing blankly over the ship's rail and shaking his head as he looked at the Pacific and said, "Chaplain, at last I've seen something bigger than Texas."

We finally reached Noumea, the port for the French island of New Caledonia. Coming off the ship, I joined those who were headed for what had been described as the longest bar in the Southwest Pacific. It was truly a bar of imposing length. At the far end I thought I saw somewhat indistinctly through the tobacco smoke the strangely familiar figure of a grey-haired Marine officer who stood head and shoulders above an admiring circle of very young second lieutenants and a mound of empty beer bottles.

Getting closer, I caught the eye of the older officer, and he seemed to recognize me as familiar. Suddenly I realized that he was a man I had known with much awe as Master Gunnery Sergeant Buckley when I was in the Platoon Leaders class at Quantico. As he later explained, he had been "demoted" to being a commissioned officer during the war. When I drew nearer to him, a big grin of recognition spread across his face, as he saw the cross on the collar of my uniform and said, as if in disbelief, "Not one of my college boys—a chaplain!"

We soon renewed our acquaintance on a somewhat different level than it had previously existed, but I still stood in awe of him, for he was one among a number of legendary Marine Master Gunnery Sergeants, anyone of whom would have made a Roman centurion look like an amateur warrior. As the evening wore on, however, he said something I have never forgotten, although it astonished me when he said it. "I want to tell you," he said, "If I had not been a Marine, I would have been a priest, but I guess I would have had trouble with Latin."

The next morning was Sunday and I would have said at least a private Mass, but my beautiful portable mass kit in its beautiful but heavy brassbound oak box lay somewhere under a vast heap of luggage. It was a gift from Gordon Wadhams and friends at the Church of the Resurrection and in exquisite taste. But like so many other Anglo-Catholic things, it was not practical. Later I learned to carry the Eucharistic necessities over my shoulder in a light canvas bag that had once contained a gas mask.

Since I could not celebrate the Eucharist myself, I decided that I would look for some Catholic mission in the area near the Transient Officers Camp where we were staying in the country outside Noumea. I had been told that there was a native village named St. Louis not far away and that there was said to be a church there. I set out to look for it accompanied by a Jewish rabbi whom I had met on the transport. He was a qualified anthropologist as well as a rabbi and had been telling me a great deal about the various groups of natives living in that part of the Pacific.

At length we met a native man who courteously directed us to the mission of St. Louis and we arrived at what turned out to be a large, well-appointed church. A Sung Mass was about to begin, with the choir consisting of the entire congregation of several hundred natives, who sang Latin Gregorian chants. After the Mass ended we talked with one of the mission priests, a man who came from a noble family in France and had served the mission for many years. My friend the rabbi asked him many questions and later admitted that Catholicism seemed to have had much more of an impact upon the local population than his reading had led him to believe.

When we finally reached the First Marine Division on the island of Pavuvu, I was assigned to the famous Fifth Regiment, which had distinguished itself earlier on Guadalcanal and had won various battle honors during the First World War at Belleau Wood and other places. I was replacing the regimental Protestant Chaplain, a Norwegian Lutheran named Ansgar Sovik. He was very happy to be able to return to the States and told me he had been praying for my safe arrival. He then assured me he would pray also that I would not be hit on the head by one of the coconuts which frequently dropped from the surrounding palm trees, at least until he was safely on his way. Indeed, the regiment was set up right in the middle of a large grove of palm trees that were said to belong to the Palmolive Soap Company.

My Roman Catholic colleague in the Fifth Regiment was Father Charles M. Eggert, a priest from St. Paul, Minnesota, who was half Irish and half Swedish. He had been ordained for about six years and had served in combat with the regiment during the recently completed Cape Gloucester campaign on New Britain. Thus, compared to me, he was a seasoned veteran. At first, we occupied separate tents, but as we became acquainted and worked together, we shared a larger tent as our common living quarters.

The First Marine Division, at the time when I joined it, was in the slow process of making Pavuvu a place more or less fit for human habitation. The island, which was but one part of an extensive coconut plantation, was mostly coral. It supported a large population of landcrabs and rats, which fed and bred in the large piles of rotting coconuts. At night the landcrabs scurried across the coral floor of the tent, while the rats ran wildly around the outside on the top, which Charlie Eggert called The Indianapolis Speedway.

Slowly a Seabee battalion built roads and cleared much of the debris. Meanwhile our colonel ordered that a chapel should be built under the direction of the chaplains, neither one of whom knew the first thing about how to build it.

Fortunately, help was near at hand. There were native villages on three nearby islands; two of these were Catholic and the other was Anglican. Charlie and I ministered to these villages on a regular basis, and after some negotiations we finally gained the help of the chiefs and their men, who had built churches for their own communities and knew well how to use the palm wood and leaves to create buildings perfectly adapted to the heat and the rains of that part of the world.

When it was completed, our new chapel was large enough to accommodate about eight hundred. It had a coral floor and was constructed of palm logs and jungle stringers. Open on the sides for ventilation, it had a double, high-pitched louvered roof made of skillfully woven palm leaf thatching. Charlie and I had separate offices and used the common altar at different hours.

Lumber to make pews had been hard to find, but with the help of prayer and a case of whiskey I managed to procure, we were able to get some nice finished lumber from the Seabees. The colonel, who could never get the lumber he needed through the usual official channels, came to our first services, sat on the new pews and declared we had performed some kind of a miracle.

On Sundays there were two services for Protestants—an early morning celebration of the Episcopal Communion Service and a later General Protestant Service of Worship. The response of the Marines was excellent and I was greatly helped by a young private named Jack Hicks, who was musically talented and played the hymns on a portable field organ. Jack was a Methodist and a very pleasant individual who also helped me with clerical work, such as records of services, baptisms, instructions, reports to the Chief of Chaplains and other such items. But he did lack the talents and survival skills of Charlie's assistant, who was known as a real "operator " and who had informed me about the possible deal with the Seabees that had resulted in our getting our pews by the use of "spirits" that were not spiritual.

During the months on Pavuvu, I interviewed most of the almost eighteen hundred men in the regiment who were listed as being Protestants. Many had, in fact, never been baptized and some were instructed by me and baptized at their request. A few even asked for instruction for Confirmation in the Episcopal Church. I did instruct them but since there were no Anglican bishops about, I had to give them certificates they could submit to be confirmed by a bishop when they went home. I remember witnessing Roman Catholic Confirmations performed by a Catholic chaplain who was not a bishop but had been given the necessary faculties for use in the wartime situation. I admired the practical Roman common sense which made this possible.

My work on Pavuvu was aided greatly by a group of very

young junior officers, some of whom were most faithful communicants of the Episcopal Church. I was only twenty-six, but the space of five years or so between these young men and myself seemed much greater; a great many of the enlisted men who came regularly to church services were, of course, eighteen or nineteen. Consequently, in my circle of young officers I was sometimes laughingly referred to as "the Grand Old Man of the Fifth Marines." It is a title I wish that I had really merited. Contrary to the myths of the period, there were, of course, some atheists both in and out of foxholes, but most of the Marines I encountered were respectful with regard to religion. This was often accompanied by personal attachment to some physical object, such as a medal of a saint. Some Protestant lads carried New Testaments covered with a steel cover that fit neatly into a dungaree pocket over their hearts.

The religious needs of the regiment took an unusual turn on one occasion when we had been informed that we were about to move out on a "blitz," which meant an assault on some Japanese-held island. The colonel called me in and told me that the Navajo Indians in the regiment wanted to hold what he described as "some kind of a war dance that they said was religious." These Navajo Marines were respected communications men. They spoke their native dialects on the field telephones and the Japanese could not translate anything that was overheard. The colonel explained that he was anxious to allow them to have their "religious war dance."

"But," he said, "we can't have that sort of thing going on in the regiment unless some chaplain is in charge of it, to make the arrangements and see that nobody bothers them. It's a religious thing, but it's not Catholic and it's not Jewish. For the Marine Corps, that means it's got to be Protestant and you are in charge of it."

Needless to say, I did as ordered and the quite impressive "religious war dance" was held without incident, with me standing by as an official observer. During the course of it, I learned that each man, in addition to his identification tags and various Christian medals, wore a small sack of earth on a chain around his neck. These sacks contained earth from the Navajo tribal land, and the belief was that the ancient gods who ruled that earth would accompany it and them into battle.

When the time came for the Division to prepare for the coming action, we went down to the big supply base on Guadalcanal to load the ships and "stage" for the invasion. Just before leaving we all sat on improvised seats in our regimental "outdoor movie theater" as a heavy tropical rain fell and the then popular film *Guadalcanal Diary* was shown on the screen. Some of those watching this Hollywood production had been in the actual fighting and they howled with laughter at what the movie people had thought it was like. When we got down to the island, however, these same men very solemnly visited the graves of their fallen friends who were buried there.

It was, of course, only when our convoy was at sea that we learned our target was the island of Peleliu in the Palau group. There was supposed to be an important airfield there, as well as at least twelve thousand Imperial Japanese Marines. This assault, we later learned, was all part of some great plan to protect the flanks of MacArthur's coming invasion of the Philippines. When that news got out, it was greeted with derisive Marine Corps profanity, for "Dugout Doug" was about as popular with the Marines as Emperor Hirohito.

The assault on Peleliu began early on September 15, 1944. I observed that it was the day dedicated to Our Lady of Sorrows. The date could not have been more appropriate.

Military historians have ranked Peleliu, a coral rock about eight miles long and three miles wide, with Tarawa and Iwo Jima among the bloodiest battles in Marine Corps history. Three days before the invasion, Admiral Halsey's Third Fleet had blasted the place and had destroyed barracks, hangars, radio stations and just about every visible target.

The trouble was that the Imperial troops were not among the visible targets upon which the Navy had hurled so much destruction. The Japanese had been fortifying the island since shortly after the First World War and their men had moved into the very face of the coral rock ridges. They had what *Life* magazine well described as "formidable, ingeniously contrived positions underground, in cliffsides and tunnels under the ridges." The coral reef, which was about seven hundred yards wide, formed a network of defense that was covered with concrete posts and railroad ties covered with barbed wire. Underwater mines circled the landing points. Mortars and artillery of all kinds were "zeroed in" on the beaches and operated from caves in the ridges. These caves had steel doors, which closed to protect the positions of the guns from aerial observers. In addition, there was the intense heat of the place, for Peleliu is on the equator and temperatures as much as one hundred and fifteen degrees Fahrenheit took a toll of men and equipment as the division struggled to gain so much as a toehold on the beach.

In combat the battle station of a Marine chaplain is with the medical personnel, usually in a forward aid station. The problem that first few hours at Peleliu was to find such an aid station. I went in with the fourth or fifth wave. We had gone down cargo nets and gotten into boats that circled around for several hours in the growing dawn, while many men managed to lose the splendid breakfast of steak and eggs that had been served at two in the morning. Finally the boats had taken us to the coral barrier reef, where armored amphibious vehicles waited. These were under fire and some were hit even as Marines transferred into them to be carried across the reef. The narrow beach was a place of death and almost total confusion.

By the time I arrived there, we had moved in no more than a hundred yards and seemed stopped with our heels close to the water. I saw no aid station and jumped into the nearest shell crater I could find. In that unlikely place, as a result of one of the hundreds of blunders of the day, I found a group of Seabees, all of whom were stevedores. One of them looked at me and said, "Chaplain, they told us we was the best stevedores in the whole South Pacific, and they promised we would never see combat. But them booms is really fallin' and that scrafnel is really flyin'. And I ask you, Where are we now?"

I was not at all sure what the answer to that was, and I ventured to peer over the rim of our refuge. What I saw was that no one was standing upright. Movement, where there was any, was by crawling and it was evident that many of the prone figures would not ever move again.

Suddenly, however, I saw someone walking calmly, slowly through the exploding confusion. Much to my chagrin I recognized the figure and unmistakable mighty chin of Charlie Eggert, who was himself looking for a medical aid station but stopping from time to time beside some fallen man. He looked perfectly composed.

Now I knew that I had to get up from that miserable hole. I could scarcely do otherwise, as I saw my Catholic colleague so evidently able to get on with what we were both supposed to be doing. Very reluctantly, and numb with a great fear, I climbed up and went dodging down the beach to where Charlie was. As I came up to him, he said, with a perfectly dead-pan, matter-of-fact expression on his face, "Well, it looks like there's somebody here other than ourselves."

He was, of course, doing his best to steady me with a bit of typical Marine black humor in the face of the surrounding evidence that there were indeed thousands of hostile troops on that island whose intention was to push the First Marine Division, or what would be left of it, back into the ocean. Yet, I do believe that deep down somewhere within him there was the assurance that even in this awful place there was Someone other than ourselves and that this assurance was what carried him forward to do that Someone's work. And there was indeed much to be done.

How much there was may be gathered from the fact that before the battle would end some forty days later there would be virtually no living Japanese troops left; we would have taken about seven thousand casualties, with almost two thousand dead, and Captain Preston Parish would be the one company commander in the Seventh Marines who was not either killed or wounded. Infantry platoons of sixty would leave the island with ten; one company of one hundred seventy-five would be reduced to thirty-six. The whole First Regiment would be literally decimated and have to be relieved after the first day.

On the day before the landing, I had given Communion to about five hundred men at a shipboard Eucharist. For the whole first week there was no chance to have any formal worship, but I was busy with burials and with the wounded and dying, for whom Unction seemed a source of strength in many instances, even for those who would not have begun to know just what was happening to them as they hovered or lapsed into unconsciousness.

After the first week, there were opportunities to offer the Eucharist in sheltered areas of battalions close to the action, but mostly for both Charlie and me it was a constant round of seeking out small groups and individuals for Holy Communion and trying to be of some help to those seriously wounded.

As we came near to the end of the campaign and the fighting was all but over, Charlie and I, together with our faithful Marine assistants, came at last to a wrecked Japanese radio station. We crawled inside and for the first time in a long time we slept under shelter. It seemed like a great luxury after all the rain-drenched foxholes where we had so often tried to get a night's rest.

After Peleliu was declared to be secured, a rumor spread that we would all be sent to Australia, as had happened when the Division had ended its first Pacific campaign on Guadalcanal. This rumor aroused many memories among our real veterans of what they used to call The Battle of Melbourne. As a chaplain on Pavuvu, I had sometimes heard echoes of that legendary time, for once in awhile my office would get a letter from some Australian woman who was trying to locate some long-gone Marine.

But the happy rumors about going to Australia died the death of military rumors generally and a transport eventually took us back to the base on Pavuvu, which by that time had reached a level of civilization so great as to enable it to boast of a Red Cross Office and compound, where it was said that there were actually females. And so there were, but that fact had little or no bearing upon the routine of the average Marine "grunt," who simply returned to his old battalion area to prepare and train for the next "blitz."

Like everyone else, I had no desire to go on another campaign. Like everyone else, I wanted to go back to the States. At times, I must admit, I even wished I was back in Bainbridge. Moreover, I had learned that three of my closest priest friends would soon be leaving for other duty. One of these was Charlie Eggert, with whom I had shared so much and from whom I had learned so much on Peleliu. Another was Father Joseph Ryan of the Eleventh Marines, who was destined to become an Archbishop and the Military Ordinary for all Catholic chaplains many years later. He had been decorated for his work on Peleliu and exemplified what struck me as the quality of quiet strength under stress which I admired but did not have in great supply.

In the Providence of God, I was not to see Joe Ryan again until August 27, 1983 when he and Charlie Eggert came to my ordination as a Catholic priest in the cathedral of the Diocese of Providence, Rhode Island.

My third friend who was among those leaving after Peleliu was the truly legendary Father Garrett Francis Xavier Murphy, the Division Senior Chaplain. A giant of a man, with sharp blue eyes and the weathered face of one who resembled many a Kerry fisherman, he was what was called a "retread" because he had served as a chaplain with Marines in the First World War and had been permitted to serve them again, with a waiver for age. His rugged frame, indeed, seemed ageless.

Few men I have known have impressed me more favorably than did Garrett Murphy. He was a maverick who defied the motto of the Chaplains School, which was "Never stick your neck out." He never hesitated to protest injustices done to enlisted men and I saw him on Peleliu when he acted to end brutality that was being inflicted on some Korean laborers who were among the very few prisoners of war. In his civilian ministry, he had been anything but popular with the then Cardinal in Philadelphia, whose rigidity he described as asinine. When he left us to go to Honolulu to become Senior Chaplain of the whole Fleet Marine Force, he promised to remember me. And he was as good as his word.

I soon learned that I had been indeed fortunate to have served with such priests as I have just described. Excellent men are rare in most groups of human beings and chaplains, whether Catholic or Protestant or Jewish, are no exception.

The most charitable thing I ever heard said about Charlie Eggert's successor as Catholic chaplain in our regiment was said to me by a Jesuit chaplain who knew him quite well. His explanation for the man's somewhat inept behavior was, "The poor guy played a good game of basketball in a high school run by some order. Then one of the brethren hit him over the head with a piece of lead pipe. By the time he came around, he was ordained."

My experience of him was that when he was not sleeping, he was either looking for food or complaining about it when he found it. From time to time also he would complain to me about the Catholic Church's lack of understanding of his problems, chief of which was his problem with celibacy. He kept telling me how lucky I was to be a Protestant and in a church in which ministers could get married. Since I had stopped writing to Mildred Cole and had stated that I had no intention of marrying her or anyone else, I did my best to convince him that he was wrong. Obviously, I failed to do so, for he not only went to sleep as I spoke to him, but after the war reportedly left the priesthood and got married.

Paired with this less than scintillating colleague, I carried on the routine of my office on Pavuvu and celebrated Christmas with what was really a beautiful Eucharist in the chapel we had built. By that time, I had trained a volunteer choir to sing the music of the Mass of the Angels and they did so that Christmas Eve, together with all the familiar carols, in such a way as to move the packed congregation to join them.

By the spring of 1945, it was evident that the war in Europe would end, as it did in May. But we anticipated that the Japanese would never surrender until after a costly invasion of their home islands in the course of which thousands on both sides would die. Their forces were clearly in retreat from the ground they had first gained, while much of their naval and air power had been destroyed in Leyte Gulf.

But the home islands, we knew, would be defended to the death. Thus when we finally learned that a new invasion was in store for us and when we went through the usual staging operations, we had a great sense of foreboding. When we left Pavuvu and headed north in convoy in March, we finally had confirmed what had been rumored: we were going to invade Okinawa, which was at least on the perimeter of Japan itself.

This sense of foreboding was increased when we joined an enormous convoy in a huge anchorage surrounded by a coral atoll. One of the ships there was the aircraft carrier *Ben Franklin*, which had been hit by a Japanese suicide pilot while the ship was loading ammunition off Okinawa. The damage and casualties had been very great, as I had the opportunity to see when I stopped at the *Franklin* while making my rounds to our own ships at the anchorage which carried Marines from the regiment but had no chaplains. This was done in a small boat and it was usually necessary to climb a rope ladder hanging down in choppy waters, where one had to jump, catch the ladder, and climb the side of the ship to be visited. Of course, we had no Marines on the *Franklin*, but I went aboard to visit a friend, who told of how the Catholic chaplain had saved lives and helped to control damage. That chaplain, incidentally, later received the Congressional Medal of Honor.

All signs and many reports of Navy casualties pointed to a very costly landing on Okinawa. We approached that island during Holy Week and there were church services every day. On Good Friday the ship's large mess hall was jammed as we reviewed the Seven Last Words of Christ from the cross. The actual landing took place on Easter morning and the Eucharist the evening before was one of the best attended services I have ever conducted anywhere. Those of us who had been at Peleliu certainly prayed extra hard.

The sight we saw that Easter morning was of a fleet that stretched beyond the horizon in seemingly endless array. We climbed into landing craft and were lowered down the side of the transport. A stiff breeze blew and cold sea water sprayed us, who had long been used to tropical temperatures. I joined in the universal shivering, but it was not cold water that had me somewhat shaking. We were waiting for the worst to happen.

There was a radio in our landing craft and we could not believe what we were hearing, as unit after unit reported landings without any opposition. Finally, in joyful disbelief we also walked onto the beach without opposition, and a young officer looked at me and said, "Padre, you must have worked a miracle."

There was reason to feel relief, but it was short-lived, for the Japanese elected to allow us to come ashore in the belief that while our supporting ships would be destroyed by suicide pilots, our advancing forces would also be destroyed by their troops, who were in very well-prepared defensive positions.

But after the first week it was evident that our ultimate victory was inevitable, except, of course, that the Japanese did not think so. There were many anxious moments, like the night I spent in an aid station with some medical corpsmen, the regimental surgeon and some wounded Marines. Outside there were a lot of new, and very nervous, replacements in the defense perimeter. Suddenly they all started shooting at something they thought they heard coming and bullets flew through the aid station. As we lay on the floor together waiting for this madness to stop, the surgeon, who was an obstetrician in civilian life, said, "They sent me to field medical school to teach me how to work with Marines. What they should have done was to send me to an insane ward where all the inmates had rifles."

That kind of humor has helped to sustain men at war ever since the Greeks took Troy. It is a kind of counterweight to the senseless nature of war itself. This senselessness is never more evident than when men go on killing and dying long after their cause is really lost. So it was that sometimes isolated Japanese snipers cut off from their units would wound some passing Marine in the hope of killing anyone who might attempt to come to his aid.

I became involved with just such a situation when a medical corpsman and I saw such a wounded Marine and started to move to his side. Had he not seen us and warned us off, we might well have fallen into the trap. Instead, we were able to bring up a couple of Marines with a machine gun that made short work of the sniper and enabled us to bring help to the wounded man. In the course of this episode, I had to do a great deal of crawling about in the mud, and was reminded of the words of the twenty-second Psalm that we had sung in the seminary chapel: "I am a worm and no man."

In the closing days of the Okinawa action and as things quieted down, I really had a chance to reflect upon the narrow escape I had had, as well as upon others when we were on Peleliu.

I had no way of knowing then that the worst was over or that it would not be long before I would find myself safe in Honolulu. But I was very sure that Charlie Eggert had spoken more truly than he knew when he had said amidst the carnage and confusion of the Peleliu beach that there was someone there other than ourselves. And that Someone evidently had something more in mind for me. My life, I knew, was in His hands.

SEVEN

How High Is Up?

When Okinawa was declared secured, the regiment got word to prepare to go to China. And I got word that Garrett Murphy had not forgotten me, but had arranged for me to get orders to go to Honolulu for the purpose of setting up a survival training course for Navy chaplains who were making the transition to service with Marine units and knew nothing about life "in the field."

I had, however, scarcely arrived when on Wednesday morning, August 15, the *Honolulu Advertiser* ran the headline "Peace At Last." Emperor Hirohito was quoted as calling the atomic bombs that had fallen on Hiroshima and Nagasaki "new and most cruel" weapons that had forced Japan to surrender.

At this distance in time, it is interesting to note something else that the Emperor said to his defeated nation: "Cultivate the ways of rectitude. Foster the nobility of spirit and work with resolution so it may enhance the innate glory of the imperial state and keep pace with the progress of the world." That his one hundred million subjects heeded his advice about keeping pace with progress, is evident from Japan's present position in the world of international finance.

But on August 15, 1945 the residents of Honolulu, who had experienced Pearl Harbor, could not have cared less about the cruelty of the atomic bombs or the future of Japan. There was, as the *Advertiser* reported, not a quiet spot in town. Certainly there was nothing quiet about the Marine Corps Transient Officers Center where I was, except in those few dark corners where Marines, overcome by celebrating, snored in peace while they rested up for renewed rejoicing.

My new assignment was the perfect "Catch–22." I had an office, an assistant, and a Jeep; but there was not any further need to teach chaplains how to survive when with Marines in combat. The bombs that were said to have destroyed sixty percent of Hiroshima and thirty percent of Nagasaki had made that problem irrelevant. Thus for over a month after the coming of peace I had the very pleasant, and very unofficial, task of helping returning young Marine officers to adapt to life among civilians, as these officers passed through on their way home.

I was aided in my activities by a Mrs. Snodgrass, who was said to be the widow of an admiral of that name. I had met this charming and generous lady at the Episcopal Cathedral after a service and during a social hour that followed. She had a fine house and swimming pool high above the city and willingly entertained some of my Marine friends and myself at pleasant parties, at which there were always young ladies from very good families in Honolulu, as well as others who had come from the States to work there in various offices during the war. At these always decorous parties, my young officers were given an opportunity to re-discover a world that they had not known for some time. It was not always easy for them to deal with the niceties of such occasions, but it did not take them long to find ways of handling that problem. They were, after all, very ingenious young Americans, who had just helped to win a war and they knew how to adapt to environmental changes.

This idyllic interlude was rather like the adventures of Odysseus in Lotos Land, for it was somehow suspended in time and seemed like an endless summer. But by October, I was not in Lotos Land but back home in Newark on a thirty-day leave before reporting for duty at the Naval Separation Center at Lido Beach on Long Island.

The trip home from San Francisco was almost as mythic as my last weeks in Honolulu had been, except that it was on a much lower social level. A few other officers and I had been given transportation back East on a train that was set up to carry four hundred Australian war brides to New York. They were a pleasant, very earthy lot; their vision of America had, however, been created by the Hollywood films they had seen and the very tall tales they had been told by American servicemen. Many of them, I am certain, must have been much disappointed when they arrived at the places they said they were going to meet their husbands and new relatives. Some of these destinations were, in fact, in certain remote rural areas which would make even the worst parts of Australia's "outback" look attractive.

Yet I had the impression that these hearty women would prove to be survivors wherever they went, for most of them were realists. Typical was the comment of one youngster from Melbourne when she looked out of the train window and saw a much-over-thirty casino hostess walking on the platform as we were stopped in Las Vegas. This woman was wearing clothing intended for one much younger and was heavily made up. Turning to me, the young girl from Melbourne said, "Eee, Chaplain, look at 'er. Now that's what we call mutton done up like lamb."

Such sharp realism was something very much needed for all of us returning home, for men at war tend often to idealize the homes they left or expect to take up their civilian lives where they had left off. But even if they do not have such illusions, their families generally find that it is sometimes difficult to see in the returning veteran the same person they once knew and had expected to see again.

For my own part, my days of leave seemed to be surrounded with unreality; our apartment, my mother, the furniture, the streets I had known just eighteen months before—all of it seemed somehow unreal. I walked around the city unsure of where things were. The people at the church, including my old rector, all seemed as if they were almost strangers.

They were, of course, more than kind and happy to see me, but when, for example, I spoke before the members of the Women's Auxiliary at the parish hall, I really found it most difficult. They were no longer "my people." My people were "Marine people," and I felt that these "civilians" had nothing in common with them.

There was also the experience of seeing Mildred Cole in a changed light. I best remembered her as a young girl standing embarrassed among her father's fluttering pigeons. After a long silence when I had been on Pavuvu, I had begun writing to her again just before we had left for Okinawa. My reason for doing so was that I had become convinced that I would probably die in that invasion. This feeling, which was not uncommon among those who had experienced the invasion of Peleliu, was really something that I more or less accepted as the realistic way to look at what to expect when invading a place so close to the Japanese home islands.

It had been in that rather fatalistic frame of mind that I had thought I should explain to her, for whatever it might be worth, that I had really cared about her more deeply than I had wanted to admit. She had replied and we had corresponded since that time more and more as two people in love, although my letters especially lacked the conventional romantic flavor most of the time.

Now that I had returned, it was evident when we met that

Mildred was not any longer as I had remembered her. Suddenly she was there, a young woman who was almost twenty, and there was no doubt in either of our minds that we were on the brink of marriage. If I had gone off to the war to escape that issue, it was clearly much more real now that I had managed not to die on Okinawa but to return to Grace Church, where the questions I had about celibacy and a clerical career were likewise no less real, but rather even more so.

The parish vestry had voted that when I returned to the staff of Grace Church, which they anticipated would happen as soon as I was released from the Navy, I should do so with the status of Associate Rector. My work as a chaplain had been glowingly reported in an Episcopalian magazine called the *Living Church* in the previous January by its editor, Clifford Morehouse, a Marine officer who visited our regiment after Peleliu. As a result, I found myself a minor Anglo-Catholic celebrity.

Indeed, my clerical career appeared to be taking off in a number of possible directions. My duties as a chaplain at the Lido Beach Separation Center gave me a great deal of free time. I lived in Newark and commuted to work, which consisted in giving a set talk to a captive audience of men who were involved in the boring, paper-ridden process by which they were moving out of the Navy world and back into the world of normal human beings. Most of my day was spent among the tormented travellers caught in the purgatorial terrors of the Long Island Railroad.

It was not at all difficult to get time off from this arduous piece of military futility, for there were far more chaplains at Lido Beach than were really needed to give the talks that could, in any case, have been given by a robot. Consequently I was able to accept various speaking and preaching invitations I received from Anglo-Catholic groups and parishes. Moreover, all my weekends were free from any military duty.

I knew, however, that I had really achieved a new summit when I was invited to preach at what was described as a Solemn Mass of Requiem for the war dead to be held at the Church of St. Mary the Virgin, which I have described earlier as "the Anglo-Catholic Cathedral," on November 12. This event was sponsored by the New York branch of an organization called the Clerical Union for the Maintenance and Defense of Catholic Principles. It featured, among other musical gems, a Celano setting of a medieval *Dies Irae* and was described in some detail by the *New York Times*, where it was stated that a flag-draped catafalque stood before the altar, at which the Mass was offered by the celebrant, deacon, and subdeacon dressed in black vestments.

Everything liturgical was done that day as much as possible in such a way as to be in accord with what was then supposed to be the best Roman style. I still recall my embarrassment when I arrived in my Navy uniform carrying a small bag in which there were the vestments I expected to wear. These consisted of a simple Roman cassock and surplice. But when I took them out in the sacristy, the Master of Ceremonies at once informed me that I would be improperly attired as the preacher if I did not wear a black mantelletta and a biretta. Since I had to confess that I had neither with me, I had to wear those provided for me out of the parish's more than ample supply.

On another occasion, I was very happy to be invited by Bill Kibitz to return to Christ Church, New Haven to preach at a service of Vespers and Benediction, at which there were to be acolytes gathered from many parishes according to an annual custom.

But from the point of view of my future life, the most important invitation I received was from Gordon Wadhams to preach at the principal Mass at his parish on Sunday, November 4, 1945. I looked forward to going there where I had visited so many times as a student when I was at Columbia and where I had been given the gift of the very handsome—if very impractical—field altar I had brought home from the war.

What I did not know was that there would be in the congregation that morning, by prearrangement, a group of gentlemen who were members of a search committee charged with finding a suitable new rector for one of the venerable fortresses of Anglo-Catholicism, St. Stephen's Church, adjacent to the campus of Brown University in Providence, Rhode Island, where, because of the amounts of incense used in its services, it was sometimes referred to as "smokey Steve's" among irreverent undergraduates.

Charles Townsend, who had served as rector of St. Stephen's since March, 1930, had recently resigned to take a less demanding, smaller parish, and had suggested that his successor should be both young and vigorous. In the practice of the Episcopal Church, which is not unlike that of other Protestant churches in the United States, the members of the vestry or lay governing board had the responsibility of finding and "calling" a rector, who might even be a priest who was canonically resident in some other diocese. In order to accomplish their task, the members of the vestry who were appointed to a search committee to find a new rector had consulted, not their bishop, but well-placed lay friends in their own social circles. Someone from New York who attended the Church of the Resurrection had urged the search committee to consider me as a possible candidate.

A more unlikely way of choosing a suitable rector could not be found even if one tried; but at least it makes it perfectly clear from the outset that the rector who accepts the "call" of the vestry will be their employee and will serve, not at the pleasure of the bishop, but at the pleasure of the more prominent laity of the parish. In this respect, as in many others, the Episcopal Church in the United States is less episcopal than its title suggests. The gentlemen who met with me after I had preached that Sunday morning during the Mass at the Church of the Resurrection were, of course, complete strangers who knew nothing about me other than what they had been told by their New York friends.

They were apparently favorably impressed because after they had introduced themselves, they invited me to come to St. Stephen's some weekend to consider, and to be considered for, the position of rector of the parish. I remember asking whether or not there were any stipulations regarding the question of marriage and was told that Father Townsend was married, as had been his predecessors. This was not, then, one of those very unusual Anglo-Catholic parishes which traditionally employed only unmarried clergy, as was the case at Grace Church, Newark.

I duly went to Providence one weekend. After saying Mass and preaching at St. Stephen's, I was interviewed and met with the members of the vestry. I did not so much as meet the Bishop of the Diocese of Rhode Island, the Right Reverend James De Wolf Perry, who was also the Presiding Bishop of the Episcopal Church and thus the Anglican Primate in the United States.

On December 17, 1945, three days after my twenty-ninth birthday, I received a telegram inviting me to become rector of St. Stephen's. It was signed by Robert H. Ives Goddard, who was the Senior Warden of the vestry, and contained— as something of an afterthought—the statement that this invitation had the approval of Bishop Perry.

I responded by saying that I was honored and would give serious consideration to the invitation but that I could not, in any case, assume the position of rector until I had been released from the Navy, which was something I anticipated in the very near future. While in the process of doing so, I was to receive a letter from Bishop Perry early in January. This letter, written in his own handwriting, informed me that if I were to decide to come to St. Stephen's, I would find a warm welcome in Providence, a place of which I knew nothing, except that it was the location of Brown University, which in my days at Columbia had been known as a great place for parties, football, and a relaxed academic atmosphere on the outer fringe of the Ivy League.

I took an inordinate amount of time before deciding to accept the invitation from St. Stephen's. I had other things on my mind, for just before her twentieth birthday, on December 2, in the very unromantic setting of Schrafft's restaurant, with its suggestions of afternoon tea and eclairs, I asked Mildred to marry me, and we set the date of December 27 for the ceremony at Grace Church. I had the feeling that I had finally come to terms with clerical life as it was in most of the Episcopal Church, and I was certain that I was about to share it with a woman who was both unpretentiously and essentially "religious," if by that term is meant a love for God, the beauty of holiness, and the Faith that was once delivered to the Apostles.

As I have said, marriage was not an obstacle to my becoming the rector of St. Stephens. But I was astonished to discover that it would not stand in the way of my becoming Associate Rector at Grace Church, where I was informed that in my case there would be no objection whatever if the tradition of celibate clergy were to be broken. Indeed, the announcement of our wedding plans, which provoked some jocular comment from some of my clerical friends, seemed to present no difficulty for anyone, except my mother. Her reaction was about like that of any widowed mother of an only son.

She, however, conceded that if I must get married, Mildred would be, as she put it, "better than most." Mildred's father, I suspect, was thinking that his daughter could have done, as he might have said, "a lot better than that." But he had the kindness not to say so, at least to me.

Our wedding, at which Father Gomph presided and Father Bill Kibitz was the best man, was really very beautiful in the splendid setting of Grace Church. Since I was still in the Navy, however, our honeymoon consisted of a weekend in New York because I had to report to Lido Beach the following Monday. We returned home to the apartment I had shared with my mother, who continued to live there. This was an arrangement that would have to be given a rating of less than perfect for the beginning of any marriage, to say nothing of one involving the context of clerical life and a basic decision regarding the opportunities offered by Grace Church and St. Stephen's. It was but the beginning of the trials which Mildred would experience in the strange new world she had entered as the wife of an Episcopal priest.

Why I finally decided to accept the invitation to become the twelfth rector of St. Stephen's is surely something known only to God, Whose hidden purpose in leading me to Providence was also leading me to the Catholic Church. Perhaps, I felt challenged to continue the much-needed restoration, which Charles Townsend had begun in 1942 after the worst years of the Depression. His had been an especially difficult era of financial struggle in the period between 1931 and 1942, when he was at last able to declare the parish free of debt and able to balance its budget. Even so, I knew that there remained much physical work to be done and that operating expenses were being barely met only because of income from endowment and the generosity of a few wealthy families.

I also knew that the three Sisters of the Holy Nativity, who

served the parish in many ways and ran its religious education program, were evidently in need of increased support,
even though I was not then fully aware of how woeful their
condition really was or how few parishoners had any understanding for or appreciation of their central life of prayer. I
may have thought I could be of some help to them.

Perhaps I went to St. Stephen's because I was drawn to
work in a university setting. When I had worked for the
S.T.M. at the General Theological Seminary, I had thought
of a seminary teaching career and I had enjoyed the teaching
side of parish life. Moreover, in the Marines I had met a
whole group of bright young officers just out of college and I
felt that this might give me some real understanding of university students, not a few of whom were, in fact, veterans.

Then there was the fact that St. Stephen's, unlike Grace
Church, had long been in the very forefront of the Anglo-
Catholic movement and was a place that had been visited by
such luminaries as Kenneth Kirk, the Bishop of Oxford; Father Gabriel Hebert of Kelham; the great Anglo-Catholic lay
leader Lord Halifax; and William Temple, who had come
there when he was Archbishop of York.

Indeed the ninth rector of St. Stephen's had been something of a legend in Anglo-Catholic clerical circles. Father
Frederic S. Penfold had become rector after having been a
chaplain in the First World War, which made me identify
with him. And the more I learned of his history at St. Stephen's, the more I felt that we were truly kindred spirits. He
battled to make the Mass central to the worship of the parish; he installed a most conspicuous confessional and got
Bishop Perry to bless it; he introduced the Confraternity of
the Blessed Sacrament, as well as the devotion of Benediction; he conducted devotions to Our Lady and adorned her
chapel; and he fought—and lost—a battle to install the Stations of the Cross, which had to wait for a later time.

A history of St. Stephen's, written for the one hundred twenty-fifth anniversary long after I had become a Catholic, did me the kindness of drawing a parallel between Fred Penfold and myself. It was a parallel of which I was conscious before becoming rector and it may well have contributed to my deciding to go to the parish where this man had fought so hard for seven very tortured years to achieve the impossible dream of transforming a nice, respectable High Episcopal place of worship into a Catholic parish. At the end of his rectorate he wrote, "A man can stand just so much, and then he breaks." I was to learn what he meant, but I did not take seven years to find out.

When I finally accepted the invitation to become a successor in the line of rectors that followed after Fred Penfold, it was, of course, with the understanding that I could not actually do so until I was out of the Navy, which happy event took place on May 22, 1946, after slightly more than three years of service.

In the interim, I spent various weekends at St. Stephen's, which was under the temporary care of a priest who was in many ways typical of the wonderful contradictions that inhabited the world of Anglo-Catholicism within the flexible boundaries of the Protestant Episcopal Church. The Reverend Doctor Robert P. Casey was then chairman of what was called the Department of Biblical Literature at Brown. His interests included all of the following: gourmet cuisine, textual New Testament criticism, patristics, ancient Armenian, psychoanalysis, Russian history and religion. He had worked on an edition of the *Vita Antonii* of Athanasius from the ancient Armenian text and was finally to end his days as a recognized scholar and teacher at Sidney Sussex College, in the University of Cambridge.

Bob Casey had an antiquarian love of elaborate liturgical ceremonies. For Palm Sunday in 1946 he planned ceremonies and music that would have done credit to a great cathedral in the middle of the fifteenth century, except that it was in the vernacular. But at a splendid lunch afterwards, he assured me that whether Jesus had ever actually risen from the dead was a matter of no great importance. What mattered was the survival of the "Christ myth," the central aspects of which were symbolized in the ancient liturgies, such as those of the Orthodox East.

His point of view, which was not at all uncommon among scholarly Anglo-Catholic clergy, was shaped by the work of such Roman Catholic Modernists as von Hugel, George Tyrell, and Loisy, to say nothing of such Protestant critics as Bultmann. It struck me then as a curious lot of contradictions and it seems no less so today when I so frequently encounter it under the euphemism of what seems to be more or less gently tolerated as Liberal Catholicism. But in 1946, of course, I had no idea that such things would ever happen where the Mass was in Latin and Thomism was taught in the seminaries.

That was where my heart was and on one occasion, shortly after coming to Providence and settling into a newly purchased rectory with Mildred and my mother, I met a man who knew it. The occasion was a civic ceremony that was held in the replica of an ancient Greek temple in the middle of Providence's public park and zoo dedicated to the memory of Roger Williams. I don't recall what we were celebrating there but it was one of those times when the American civic religion used to think it proper to have at least one Protestant and one Catholic clergyman present to offer prayer to the Supreme Being. As I walked up on the platform, someone grabbed my arm and said, "What the hell are you doing here?"

I turned and was astonished to see the very familiar rotund figure of Father Joe Lamb, a Catholic priest I had known as a very genial host at a Naval hospital in the Russells where weary Catholic Marine chaplains were always welcomed in Joe's quarters and I was kindly included among them. I had forgotten that Joe came from Rhode Island. Seeing him that day was like meeting a fellow countryman in a strange, foreign land.

"Why Joe," I said, all dressed in black and with a Roman collar, "I'm here to represent the Protestants."

Joe started laughing, and I joined him, as he said, "And why couldn't they get one of their own to represent them?" It was really a very proper question, for I was really not "one of their own." I was, in fact, as Matthew Arnold once wrote, a man "between two worlds"—the world of the Episcopal Church as it was and the world of Roman Catholicism, as I imagined it to be.

It is, therefore, not difficult to understand why my three years as rector of St. Stephen's were stressful, although I do not think they seemed so to most of the parishoners. The financial picture improved somewhat, and the official parish history generously credits me for doing much to revitalize the life of the parish, especially with regard to the program of religious education and work with Brown students. I was, moreover, very ably assisted by my curate Warren R. Ward, whom I had known as a seminarian from Grace Church, Newark, and whom I had invited to join me in Providence. Warren had a genial personality and what has been called "the common touch." He was able to reach out to many segments of the parish that might previously have been neglected, such as high school students and young married couples.

Indeed, apart from the fact that I felt it prudent to ask Bob Casey to move his unlicensed "psychoanalytic practice" out of the clergy quarters, the scene at St. Stephen's was generally improving and free from any serious difficulties. Things at the rectory were, however, anything but easy. Having my mother in the house complicated matters for my very young bride, who also had to cope with the kinds of problems that afflict the wives of clergymen. Her clothes, her furniture, her entertaining, her associations—all of these were subject to the constant scrutiny and comment of female parishoners. And when we had had a son and a daughter in the first two years, with a third child on the way in the third year, there were those who suggested that this was the sort of thing that happened among Roman Catholics. Proper Anglicans were more prudent in their family planning.

I did not realize it then but I certainly was very difficult to live with. I was constantly restless and often ate and drank to excess. Many nights I was shaken by dreams about the war and the harrowing experiences of those nights when the Japanese prowled around our positions during the early days of the campaign on Peleliu. On at least one occasion, I took a loaded rifle and went out in the middle of the night in pursuit of someone who had attempted to break into the kitchen. The police, who had been summoned, were less anxious to encounter this nocturnal prowler; they were understandably more anxious to have me put the rifle away and go back to bed.

My experience as a military chaplain had, as I have already said, caused me to have a place of some prominence among the younger Anglo-Catholic clergy. And St. Stephen's, with its history of leadership, was regarded as a resource for efforts to promote Anglo-Catholicism by a group called the American Church Union after the older Anglo-Catholic English Church Union. Thus it was that from October 7 to October 25 in 1947 I was an invited speaker at a series of ACU-sponsored "Catholic Congresses" in Washington, Chicago, Atlanta, Dallas, Denver, and Los Angeles. Consequently, I gained an awareness of the state of Anglo-Catholic activity in very different sections of the country.

The following year, when the Anglican bishops were

holding their 1948 meeting at Lambeth, I was invited to be a delegate of the ACU at what was billed as an International Priests' Convention sponsored by the English Church Union. The presiding officer of this gathering was to be Kenneth Kirk, the scholarly Bishop of Oxford. I was very pleased to have been invited and the parish generously made it possible for me to attend.

The place of our meeting was Farnham Castle, the residence of the Bishop of Guilford. Three sessions were held each day from June 21 through June 25. There were fifty-two priests and a scattering of bishops from fifteen Anglican provinces located in sixteen different countries. All participants represented the Anglo-Catholic movement in their respective areas. Some were noted scholars, like Gregory Dix of Nashdom Abbey; some were representative of centers of study, like Frederick Hood of Pusey House, Oxford; others were representative of religious orders, such as Father Hebert of Kelham. Others, like myself, were parish priests, like the colorful John Shand, the vicar of an industrial parish in the Episcopal Church of Scotland. Others were missionaries from Asia or Africa.

The central concern was the direction being taken at that time by the ecumenical movement, and the immediate crisis was the one afflicting the Anglican world that year. The question was what to do about something called the Church of South India, which was a sort of experimental stew made up of various Protestant missionary churches in India, in which some Anglican bishops were involved. Since this called for their accepting non-episcopal ministries, at least in the initial phases, there were many Anglicans in India who preferred not to be part of it.

And Anglo-Catholics everywhere did not want the bishops gathering at Lambeth to legitimize something which would throw into question their belief in Apostolic Succession as necessary to the ministry. As is always the case when such issues arise, there was dire talk of widespread defections to Rome if the Lambeth meeting did not heed the wishes of those of us spokesmen for the Anglo-Catholic point of view.

The bishops at Lambeth responded in the equivocal fashion in which they normally respond to issues; that is, of course, said to be the very genius of Anglicanism. They expected that somehow validly ordained bishops would finally emerge in the Church of South India after a brief interim of the mutual recognition of the ministries of all concerned. But they expressed the pious hope that this new conglomorate would somehow revise its first written constitution so as to allay some people's "doubt and anxiety" as to what was actually the faith and the practice of the Church of South India. The Anglicans in South India who wanted not to leave their Anglican allegiance had asked for a bishop to be sent to them to replace the men who had joined the new conglomorate. Lambeth denied their request, which was the one really clear thing it did that year. And it goes without saying, that the dire threats of defections to Rome on a large scale never materialized. They never do.

Equivocal as were the statements from Lambeth, nothing has ever more dramatized for me the curious dilemma of Anglicanism than did my conversation with the vicar of a prominent Anglo-Catholic parish in London, where I had gone after the Farnham meeting. I had been told that this parish was a place where I could say Mass daily while in the British capital.

The vicar, whose name was Stephen Langton, was most hospitable and assured me that I might "have an altar" each day. As we chatted over a glass of warm British gin on that hot summer morning, I asked him what liturgical book I might find in his church and mentioned several of the standard unofficial Anglo-Catholic "revisions" of the *Book of Common Prayer*.

With that he exploded, *"Book of Common Prayer!* God forbid that we should have that Protestant thing in this church. Don't you know, Father, that there is but one book that has truly canonical and ecclesiastical status in England?" "What book is that?" I asked in all my American innocence. "Why, the Roman Missal, of course," he responded at once and with great firmness. Then he added, *"The Book of Common Prayer* is a civil document that has been imposed upon the Church by Parliament. You will find the Roman Missal on our altars."

And that is exactly what I did find, the *Missale Romanum,* as decreed by the Council of Trent, put into effect by Pius V, with some later revisions under Pius X and Benedict XV. Mass there was said in Latin, just as I discovered was the case with the monastic liturgy at the Anglican Nashdom Abbey where I visited, as had Damasus Winzen who loved to tell of going there to hear how Gregorian chant sounded in the vernacular, which he favored, only to hear the Anglican monks chanting away in Latin. There were those in England who were not impressed by Thomas Cranmer's incomparable prose when it first appeared in the sixteenth century and there continued to be those in the twentieth century who shared their reaction.

As I reflected on the matter, I concluded that the London vicar was following, in a bizarre fashion, the principle of private judgment upon which so much of the Protestant Reformation was founded, even though this ironically led him to simulate the Roman Mass in a Reformation church. This was something Anglican and therefore beyond logic, like the head of Thomas More, martyred under Henry VIII for opposing the Act of Royal Supremacy, but now buried in St. Dunstan's Anglican Church in Canterbury beneath a Latin inscription calling for freedom for the Church of England.

After returning to Providence after the International Priests' Convention, visits to Nashdom, Pusey House, and a number of other places of Anglican worship and thought, I began to think of the Anglo-Catholic movement as really the product of what had been in many ways an aspect of nineteenth century Romanticism, in the form of nostalgia for a patristic past, a Christianity of the first five or six centuries which had never really existed as the Oxford Tractarians had dreamed. Their vision had far greater attraction than that of a liturgy and a Bench of Bishops set up by Parliament and under the Crown. They were appalled, as had been John Wesley, by the deadly, dull rationalism of most of the Establishment. They viewed it as moribund, but what they sought to revive had long ago fled the Church of England.

John Henry Newman, of course, had come to the conclusion, as he wrote in 1850, that anyone who studied the evidence of the Fathers and the whole patristic age as it really was could not but conclude that the history of the development of doctrine supports the continuity of the Roman Catholic Church with the Catholic Church of the early centuries, the Church described by Irenaeus, Ignatius of Antioch, Clement of Rome, and Justin the Martyr. Indeed, the conclusion of the Protestant Paul Tillich, in his book on the history of Christian thought, now seemed to me to be inescapable: if one wished to belong to a church in the modern world that would be most like that of the early centuries, one would simply have to become a Roman Catholic.

That thesis, or one much like it, became an almost constant topic of discussion among the clergy with whom I was most close. As I look back on those days, I realize that the Anglo-Catholic cause was already lost in a Church that was moving then to embrace the situation ethics later made popular by the writings of Joseph Fletcher. It was inevitable that there would come a time, like the present, when the Episcopal Church would justify abortion and homosexuality as acceptable forms of Christian behavior.

Of course, there were endless discussions about the complex question of Anglican orders, which Leo XIII's *Apostolicae Curae* in 1896 had declared to be null and void. Whatever else might be said on the subject it could not be denied that Thomas Cranmer had succeeded in eliminating the whole concept of a sacrificing priesthood from his *Book of Common Prayer* and that those who insisted that their Anglican ordinations had made them priests empowered to offer the Sacrifice of the Mass were simply rejecting the plain evidence. There was not then, of course, any talk of the ordination of women among Anglo-Catholics. Discussion dealt with the validity of Anglican ordinations, which is the basic issue in any event. Those Anglo-Catholics who may have chosen to leave the Episcopal Church in recent times because that Church has priestesses would do well, if they have become Roman Catholics, to view validity as the more basic issue. In spite of such writers as Hans Kung and F.J. van Beeck, the fact is that the position of Leo XIII remains the position of the Catholic Church, to say nothing of the Orthodox. Therefore, if Anglicans cannot confer valid orders, it matters little if they ordain priestesses, except that by these simulated ordinations they are once more providing evidence that what they are doing is far indeed from what the Catholic Church intends to do when it ordains priests.

In many of our clerical discussions of the future of the Anglo-Catholic movement which were held in St. Stephen's rectory, Mildred listened but said little. When, however, the discussions would end with the conclusion that sooner or later the Anglo-Catholics would have to become Roman Catholics, she would say, "Well, if that's the way it's going to be, why don't we become Catholics now?"

By the summer of 1949 we both knew that this was indeed the question to which we would, in all honesty, have to find the answer. Having written my S.T.M. thesis about St. Thomas Aquinas, I was interested to learn that, as someone said at a dinner party, there was "some little Catholic college run by Dominican priests on the other side of town." I then discovered that these Dominican priests, who belonged to the same order as did St. Thomas, offered philosophy courses in a summer session. Never having had a course in formal logic and never having so much as heard of "rational psychology," I decided to take courses in both those subjects at the "little Catholic college on the other side of town," which was called Providence College.

The Dominican friar who taught these courses was a tall, relatively young man of Hungarian ancestry named Joseph Jurasko. I remember having been impressed so much by his unassuming and evident sheer goodness that after the first class I came home and said to Mildred, "I don't know, but I think that I have met the real thing."

After a bit, I felt impelled to tell Joe Jurasko that both my wife and I had a question as to whether or not we ought to become Catholics. I went on to tell him of a number of books I had read about the Catholic Church. His response was to suggest that what we ought to do was to pray the Rosary for a specified period of time with the intention of receiving an answer to our problem.

I was at first put off by this seemingly naive idea, although we were familiar enough with the devotion of the Rosary, which was not uncommon among the religious exercises of some of the more "advanced" Anglo-Catholics. After some hesitation on my part, we agreed that we would each follow Joe Jurasko's suggestion during the first part of August, but not ten days had passed before we both knew the answer. Indeed when our third child was born on August 12, the next day the doctor asked Mildred when she was going on her trip because under the anesthetic at the time of the child's delivery she had kept saying, "We are going to Rome."

Fortunately, the month of August was my vacation time and Warren Ward was carrying on the work and the services at St. Stephen's, while I kept running back and forth from Providence to Cape Cod, where I was functioning as Protestant chaplain to a Rhode Island National Guard unit on summer training at Camp Edwards. There I was not required to celebrate the Eucharist, which was something I had determined not to do in the light of the decision we had made. We were undergoing instructions to become Catholics and found, as we had expected, that everything was very familiar to us.

I requested a meeting with the Roman Catholic Bishop of Providence, Russell J. McVinney, who received me with much understanding and, when I told him that we were in the process of taking instructions, he suggested that I should no longer "simulate the Eucharist." I assured him that I had already decided on that course of action, for I had accepted the judgment of Leo XIII on the subject of Anglican orders and was preparing to resign my position as rector of St. Stephen's Church, even though I had no idea of where I could find employment. The Bishop offered to help and when I suggested that I might be considered qualified to teach English, he spoke of the possibility of my going to Seton Hall University or even to Providence College.

It was not until September 12 that we were received into the Catholic Church by Father Jurasko at the Dominican Church of St. Pius. Prior to that, a most unfortunate episode took place when I had confided to Warren Ward and a mutual clerical friend that I intended to resign from St. Stephen's shortly in order to become a Roman Catholic. I did this because both of these men had been among those who had often discussed this very idea with me and had even given me reason to believe that they would follow me in the step I was about to take.

Evidently, my confidence was misplaced, for I was deeply distressed to learn while at Camp Edwards that both the Episcopal Bishop Granville Gaylord Bennett and the vestry of St. Stephens had been informed of my forthcoming resignation and the reason for it. This, of course, created an unnecessary awkwardness for all concerned and in some way aroused the interest of the local newspaper, the *Providence Journal*, which was known in Catholic circles as "The Protestant Journal." In this publication the subject of my forthcoming conversion to Catholicism became something of a ten days' wonder. But this did not cause me as much regret as did the fact that the vestry had been told that I had made something described as a "submission" to Bishop McVinney prior to giving them my resignation. This totally erroneous idea clouded my departure from St. Stephen's and offended many of the friends I had made there, as it made my actual notification of Bishop Bennett and my formal resignation both awkward and painful. But at least these things were accomplished before the end of my vacation period, during which I had not conducted any services at St. Stephen's.

My family and I were able to leave the rectory, as we were required to do, by September 1 because some very kind Catholic people were willing to rent us a house. Thus by the time we actually were received into the Church with our children we had found a home.

We not only found a home, but I found a job. We very much wanted to stay in Rhode Island to bear witness to the Faith, and were consequently delighted when the Very Reverend Robert Slavin, the President of Providence College, offered me a position as an Instructor in the English Department there. The salary was necessarily very modest, but Father Slavin and the whole Dominican community of what was then more than one hundred priests, received us with kindness, friendship, and true generosity. Thus Providence

College became the place where I would work throughout the next thirty and more years.

Talking with me about my work in Catholic higher education during those years, a President of Brown University asked me if I would please explain to him how I could have left St. Stephen's to become a Roman Catholic. I avoided giving a lecture on the mysteries of grace by saying, "I guess it was just too High Church for me." It was, perhaps, a somewhat facetious answer. But there was truth in it. St. Stephen's was surely very, very High Church, but our leaving there happened because we believed that we had heard the words, "Friends, come up higher."

EIGHT
Running With the Hounds

When my family and I became Catholics in 1949 we understood that we were converts. No one so much as suggested that we were formerly separated brethren who were now coming into full communion with the Roman Catholic Church. In those days, what is more, there were converts all over the place. Asked to contribute the story of our conversion to a volume of such stories that was originally published in German, I found myself in the company of a Russian Orthodox bishop, the former editor of an English Communist newspaper, and an assortment of artists, economists, historians and diplomats from such diverse places as Finland, India, Hungary, Germany, and Basutoland. In the following year, there were 121,950 converts received into the Church in the United States. And in the decade just before Vatican II, in Germany and England there was an average of over 10,000 converts every year.

In the Church to which we were converted, Pius XII was the Pope. The Mass of the Latin rite was in Latin everywhere, and people were attracted to Catholicism as an island of order in a very disordered world. There was no lack of priests in the United States and seminaries were flourishing, while Catholic parochial schools, staffed by religious, were the envy of Protestants and offered a challenge of excellence to the mediocrity of public education. Almost everyone in America listened to Fulton Sheen and saw his dynamic personality on television, while it seemed that Thomas Merton had revivified monastic life almost all by himself. That, of course, was before the great age of renewal in which we now find ourselves.

At this distance, it is difficult to recall those times. Indeed, it is almost easier to recall the Middle Ages as one has read of them in history books. But that is, perhaps, because one did not live in the Middle Ages, which we know only through the long perspective of time. But one thing I do remember most vividly: the genuine joy and enthusiasm there was among converts. The so-called "cradle Catholics" may have found this more than strange, but they always seemed interested in how or why conversions had taken place. In the United States, the children of the Catholic immigrant generations were even then moving towards the assimilation patterns shortly to be glamorized by the Kennedys of Massachusetts. Many of them, therefore, were mystified by such notables as Clare Luce and others who, by becoming Catholics, seemed to be rejecting the privileged White Anglo-Saxon Protestant culture, which was supposedly the model for success in America.

The enthusiasm of converts and the interest they aroused among Catholics resulted in a flood of books about conversions and produced a whole generation of speakers for Catholic organizations and the then-popular Communion Breakfasts. This reached even into my own life and I found myself during many evenings and on almost every weekend telling people who had just been to Mass and who had joined together for breakfast about how the faith of Rome was—and always had been—the one real answer to the world's problems.

It was on one such occasion that I found myself as the after-breakfast speaker in a French-Canadian parish, of which Rhode Island has quite a few. After the program ended, the toastmaster took me aside to inform me that I had been of such great interest to the men of Le Cercle Jacques Cartier that in sponsoring me as the speaker, they had voted to make an exception to one of their ethnic customs.

Looking at me quite solemnly, this gentleman said, "You are the first Irishman ever to speak before us." When I told him that I was not really Irish, he said, "But you speak English and you are a Catholic, that makes you Irish around here."

Of course, I was not always talking at Catholic tribal gatherings. I was attempting to do my job as an Instructor in English at Providence College, where I taught both the regular undergraduates and also Evening School students. Most of my students came from families in which they were the first members to attempt to get a college education. The college bulletin had informed their parents that while the faculty mostly consisted of members of the Dominican Order, a very few "carefully selected" laymen were on the teaching staff, presumably to teach courses for which no Dominican could be found.

There were no women in the teaching staff and there were no women in the student body, for single-sex institutions at the secondary and college levels were the Catholic norm in 1949 and, like most of its peers among the male institutions, Providence College was generally conceived of as a place where poor boys from Irish or Italian or French-Canadian families might start on the way to becoming lawyers, doctors, or successful businessmen. Some even thought of becoming priests.

The really unique thing about the college was that it was the only such institution for men operated by Dominicans in the United States. Unlike the Jesuits, the Dominicans were really not prepared to run colleges, although they had a tradition of university teaching extending back to the thirteenth century. At the time I joined the faculty as a newly converted layman, there were about seventy Dominicans on the faculty, with more in various administrative positions. There were about twenty laymen on the teaching staff, most of whom were part-time.

None of the Dominicans held an academic rank, but all were called professors. And none was paid a salary. Students were required to study large amounts of Thomistic philosophy and theology, and these departments were staffed and run entirely by Dominicans. Indeed all of the college administrators of any possible consequence were Dominicans, but the President really ran the entire institution and was, in addition, Superior of the religious community at the same time.

This large concentration of Dominicans under centralized administrative control meant that operating expenses were also very much under control. Thus, in accordance with the real mission of the college, the Dominicans made it possible for their students to receive both instruction in the Faith and preparation for the professional education they hoped to undertake. Tuition was $175.00 per semester and the minority who lived on campus had room and board for $275.00 per semester. There were generous scholarships available and many, if not most, of the students had jobs; some of them worked full time and at least one I knew was a Providence policeman, who brought his pistol to class.

It is said that when the noted novelist and Catholic convert Evelyn Waugh visited the United States, he remarked that he supposed that "these American Catholic colleges" existed for the purpose of "transforming a proletariat into a bourgeoisie."

The remark was typically snobbish, but it also was close to the truth. How well Providence College did this job after its founding in 1917 is suggested by the fact that in 1980 at least a third of the doctors and lawyers in Rhode Island were among its graduates. Moreover, in 1989 when tuition was $10,150 per year and room and board cost about $6,000, a very high percentage of the student body—now made up of men and women—came from alumni families, which indicates that such families are among the bourgeoisie. Such figures can, of course, be cited for most American Catholic colleges with substantial enrollments and the fact that Catholic college graduates do well among the bourgeoisie is well documented. But it is unhappily also reflected in the fact that so few of them choose poverty, chastity, and obedience, for the vows of the religious life run counter to the bourgeois grain that dominates America.

Back in 1949, of course, the college still produced quite a few vocations for the Dominican Province of St. Joseph, with its headquarters in New York, which was the Province under whose auspices the college operated. Most of those who were assigned to the faculty had probably not intended to have teaching careers, except in philosophy or theology. If they had doctoral degrees, they were in the so-called "sacred sciences," with a very few notable exceptions. One of these was a Dominican who had earned a doctorate in chemistry at Yale. So unusual was this that when he returned to New York, after some years of hard study associated with that degree, his Provincial asked him where he had been since he had not seen him for quite awhile.

Another exception was the Chairman of the English Department, whose very recent doctorate was also from Yale. My only qualification for teaching in that subject was that I had been an English major at Columbia, but my memory of the English faculty there caused me to feel keenly the need to better qualify myself for teaching college students. Consequently, in addition to teaching composition and a survey of English literature "from Beowulf to Virginia Woolf," I undertook a Masters program at Brown. I began part-time graduate study in 1950 with the aid of the G.I. Bill's educational benefits and was finally able to complete my doctorate there in 1956, with a thesis on Francis Thompson, whose well-known poem "The Hound of Heaven" appealed to me with its image of the grace of God as a hound that pursues and overtakes its quarry. Indeed, I had become fond of referring to the Dominicans as "the Hounds of the Lord" because it was through their help that we had become Catholics.

But it was God's Providence working through a Jesuit that made it possible for me to have Thompson as my thesis topic. While I was still a graduate student, I had been invited to give a talk on the poet's work before a parish book club. When I arrived for dinner at the rectory beforehand, I was astounded to be introduced to another guest, Father Terence Connolly, S.J., who was the absolute authority on Thompson and who informed me that he was looking forward to hearing my talk. The talk was a paltry thing, but Terence Connelly was a great and gracious scholar. He made available to me the extensive collection of Thompson notebooks and manuscripts he had gathered at Boston College and the result was not only my dissertation but a critical biography of Thompson, which was published in 1960.

Meanwhile, of course, I had been "running with the Hounds of Heaven" at Providence College, where in 1955 I attained the status of an Associate Professor as the result of the action of the President, who made all appointments and promotions in those days without the benefit of any academic committees. My family had grown to six children and it seemed that we needed a new house every two years or so. Five of our children were girls and two or three special friends among the Dominicans, who visited quite frequently, were fond of saying to me, "Blessed are you among women."

Mildred, in addition to caring for the children, typing my papers, and creating wonderful meals, also found time to do volunteer work at the Museum of the Rhode Island School of Design and was finally employed there as secretary to the Director for several years. Sometimes my mother, who had also become a Catholic, stayed with us, while at other times she had her own apartment. Although in failing health, to the end of her life in 1963 she found strength in the Faith and confided to me that she would have become a Catholic many years earlier but had not done so because of my being an Episcopal priest.

It was in this period, just nine years after going to work at Providence College, that I was appointed by Father Slavin to the position of Director of the Liberal Arts Honors Program, with his assurance that I would have his full confidence and support as the first layman ever to hold such administrative responsibility under his presidency.

This appointment was indeed innovative at Providence College, as was the whole idea of the Liberal Arts Honors Program for which I was now to do the necessary developmental and administrative work. Just to make sure, however, that things went well, I was given, supposedly as an assistant, a young Dominican named John Cunningham, with whom I was to have a long and happy association.

Our responsibility was to plan a program that would serve the needs of talented liberal arts students; another program for outstanding students in the sciences was in the process of development and was to be funded by the National Institutes of Health. Such programs were proliferating everywhere after the Russians sent up Sputnik I in 1957, when it was felt, at least for a time, that America was in peril of falling behind the Soviets because our schools neglected talent. This short-lived interest in academic excellence was soon to be condemned as elitism, which was a word almost as bad as sexism or racism in a society where mediocrity was supposed to be the sign of democracy.

I served as Director of the Liberal Arts Honors Program, which still exists at Providence College, for seven years and introduced the seminar method of instruction, which was a great innovation in a school where uninterrupted lectures were the usual order of the day and one sometimes had the feeling that, as someone has said, information passed from the notes of the lecturer to the notes of the student without ever going through the mind of either one.

John Cunningham and I ran the major honors seminar together in a room intended for board meetings and dedicated to the memory of former college baseball players. It became our practice to invite guests to the seminars who were persons that were expert in the topic to be discussed. Some of these provided unexpected educational experiences, not only for the students but also for their two teachers.

There was, for example, the time when the topic of the seminar was the Koran, which we had been reading the previous week. Our guest was lecturing at Harvard, where he had earned his doctorate, and was on leave from the university in Teheran, where he taught the history of science. He was a Muslim and known to have a sophisticated knowledge of his religion and its holy book. One of our students, who had learned to ask the "right" questions of visiting experts, inquired of our guest as to the sources of the Koran, with the expectation of hearing something about how Muhammad had been influenced by Judaism and Nestorian

Christianity. Instead, our sophisticated, Harvard-educated guest looked the young man straight in the eye and informed him most firmly that the source of the *Koran* was none other than Allah. At that moment all of us were reminded that there are, even in this century, learned men of faith who simply will not play academic games when confronted by the most fundamental issues.

In addition to my work in such seminars and my regular teaching assignments in the English Department, I had the experience of becoming a part-time speech writer for a veteran Congressman from Rhode Island's Second District, John Edward Fogarty, who was then chairman of the House Subcommittee on Appropriations for Health, Education, and Welfare. I was introduced to the Congressman late in 1959 in an Italian restaurant where I was having dinner with a mutual friend. Over a large plate of spaghetti, John Fogarty looked at me and said he had heard that I was supposed to be "pretty good at making speeches" and would I be interested in writing some for him.

Having always been interested in politics since my boyhood experience of the Al Smith campaign, I knew that John Fogarty was identified with aid for education and the funding of the work of medical research. I also knew that he had a labor background as a former bricklayer. That he was an Irish Catholic did not require research to discover. I quickly agreed to do some speeches and I very soon learned the valuable lesson that the true business of American political parties is not to win ideological battles but to win elections.

John Fogarty was a tough, complex, powerful personality who certainly knew how to win elections. The power his political victories gave him was, however, directed, in part at least, to serve purposes closely related to his Catholic faith, as he understood and practiced it. For example, his intense interest in funding programs for his "special kids," as he referred to mentally retarded children, began when the great Cardinal Cushing of Boston personally pointed out to him the enormous need for this work of mercy. Much of his belief in social justice was influenced not only by his background in the union to which he belonged but also to the papal social encyclicals. Of course, as he explained to me, one had to understand that getting Congress to do what he believed was right took a good deal of logrolling, which he supposed that Popes and Cardinals probably did not realize. Of course, he did not know many of them.

I suppose that the high point of my involvement with John Fogarty was the election of John Kennedy as President. They were close friends and the new President could not have had a more loyal supporter than he had in the Rhode Island Congressman. On the day when Kennedy's victory was assured, I felt proud to have been a part of the election campaign and grateful that, as it then seemed, the memory of Al Smith had been vindicated, as well as the civic loyalty of every Catholic in America.

If that was the high point, the darkest hour was on November 22, 1963 when I was called to meet with John Fogarty at his Providence office to prepare a statement to be issued to the press as the Congressman's reaction to the news that the young President had been killed in Dallas and that Lyndon Johnson, of all people, was now the Chief Exectutive. John truly needed a speech writer that day, for he was literally speechless with both sorrow and anger for what this meant for America.

Two years before that tragic day we at Providence College had suffered our own great loss in the death of Father Robert Slavin, who had been the college President since 1947 and the only one I had known. His death marked the ending of an era of absolute centralized authority and was, in some ways, a kind of foretaste of what was coming in the Church. Had he lived to learn of the calling of Vatican II, Robert Slavin would, I think, have agreed with his friend Bishop Russell McVinney, who was reported to have said on his way to the first session in 1962, "What I say is, when you have a winning team, why change?" To all the new talk of collegiality, he might well have quoted a remark attributed to Cardinal Ottaviani to the effect that the first collegial action reported in the Gospels is described in the text, "They all forsook him and fled."

Of course, at Providence College in the fall of 1962 none of us had any idea of what would come out of the impending gathering of the bishops in Rome. That was still the period when we had a compulsory annual retreat; when Dominican rectors ruled the dormitories; when many religious feast days were also college holidays; and when the academic year began with a "Red Mass" of the Holy Ghost, which was celebrated either by, or in the presence of, Bishop McVinney, who customarily addressed the students.

About to leave for the Council, as the academic year opened in 1962, the Bishop explained to the faculty and students that in the distant past, ecumenical councils had been very important. To prove this point, he cited the Sixth Council held at Constantinople in 681, when the Council had condemned the heresy of Monotheism! This unfortunate misreading of his text, where the correct term of Monothelitism appeared, provoked not the least laughter, except for the quickly suppressed convulsions of a few alert theologians.

The Bishop went on to assure us, however, that it was unlikely that this new Council would do anything very remarkable. We got the impression that it was mostly a chance for the bishops to meet the jovial Pope John XXIII, who was a pleasant interim figure. Indeed, as we left the place where the Mass had been celebrated, the Chairman of the Department of Theology commented to me that the biggest thing the Council might do was to raise the seat money collected in church to thirty-five cents.

That things turned out quite differently in Rome, was for many former Anglicans, including myself, what at first appeared to be an unmitigated disaster. I recall meeting a former parishoner of St. Stephen's who had become a Catholic about the same time that I had. We encountered one another under a tree near Brown University, just after the Council had finally ended.

The lady in question, who was a very feisty eighty years of age, said, "From what I can gather about that meeting in Rome it looks like we are going to have Mass in English, married priests, Bible schools, lots of hymns in church. Nobody will have to go to confession or eat fish on Friday. What I want to ask you is: Why didn't we stay where we were? At St. Stephen's you offered the Mass to God and didn't stand behind the altar looking at us like some fancy bartender."

I tried to tell her that all she had said was not quite accurate and made some apologetic noises about returning to ancient liturgical practices. But when I said that we still had the Pope to keep our house in order, she observed that Pope John had opened a nest of hornets and that it looked as if Pope Paul was the one who got stung.

At the time, I thought she had summed up the situation more or less correctly. Yet I did not share the view of some that the work of the Council had been dominated by members of an international Modernist plot, who were leading us all into the jungles of rationalism where ponderous German theologians trumpeted like elephants in the gloom.

But just as those who said they were "liberals" were celebrating something called "the Spirit of Vatican II," before they had so much as read its documents, so I was generally depressed by the press reports and the famous *New Yorker* articles, even though I also had not read a single official document. Having, however, lived for thirteen years as lay people in the Catholic Church, my wife and I had found it to be the Household of Faith in which we were at home and raising a family that now had grown to seven children.

Indeed, I had even published a book about the history, doctrine and organization of the pre-Conciliar Church. This book was called *Why I Am a Catholic* and was intended for the information of non-Catholics. It was an expression of my conviction that the Church to which I had been converted was that founded by Christ; the center of unity for His faithful; the extension of His Incarnation; and the unchanging witness to the Risen Lord.

I knew perfectly well that it was also tolerant of superstition; that it was sometimes disfigured by devotional extravagances, garish statuary, pious pablum, and sentimental music. That it had survived the faults of many of its leaders and managed to produce astonishing saints, whom it frequently abused in their lifetimes, was a source of wonderment. That people continued to attend Mass in large numbers in spite of indifferent or positively dreadful preaching; that they endured music which, unlike the sermons, they could not ignore; and that they were encouraging many of their children to seek religious vocations in spite of the consumer society we lived in—all those things seemed to me to bear witness to the fact that the Church must be sustained by God. But there were times when I agreed with Coventry Patmore, who is supposed to have said that he found the Faith consoling, but the faithful unendurable.

Perhaps the thing that gave me cause to be troubled about what seemed to be happening to the Church during the Council was, more than anything else, the phenomenon that came to be called "ecumenism," which at first appeared to be an almost frantic desire to "dialogue" with anyone, including atheists, who would take the time to do so.

The so-called Ecumenical Movement had been, before the Council, mostly a sort of Pan-Protestant affair. It had begun among Protestant missionaries in the nineteenth century, who, coming somewhat late upon the scene, found their divisions rather embarrassing before the heathen on the one hand and the often long-established missionaries of Rome on the other. It grew rapidly in some areas, especially among liberal Protestants, as it became more apparent in the twentieth century that the strong beliefs which had divided their forefathers no longer mattered to them. Thus it was really a liberal Pan-Protestant movement, which certainly did not interest Fundamentalists. And prior to Vatican II it seemed to be viewed by Rome with at most a detached interest. When Catholics kept their Church Unity Octave, it was to pray for the conversion of those who called themselves Christians but were separated from the One True Church.

It had always seemed to me, at any rate, that the unity of the Catholic Church was like the unity of a great classic symphony, while Liberal Protestantism resembled the cacaphony of tentative sounds in much formless modern music and the Fundamentalists were a blaring brass band endlessly playing "Stand Up, Stand Up for Jesus" in a tent back in the days before the triumphs of vulgarity achieved by TV evangelists.

Consequently, it distressed me to learn that some of the same "mainline" Protestants, whose so-called World Conferences at Stockholm, Lausanne, Edinburgh, and Amsterdam could not so much as agree on many fundamental issues, should now be invited to Rome as recognized observers at an Ecumenical Council of the Catholic Church. I had the impression that in this regard the Church was behaving like an aging dowager Duchess who, having lost track of reality, had invited for cocktails, if not for dinner, a group of distant relatives who were parlor radicals. These guests could not agree as to what form a future Socialism should take, but they were all on record as saying that there was no place any longer for dowagers, especially those with titles.

Thus in the entire period when the Council was doing its work in the years 1962 to 1965, I was less than enthusiatic about it. If someone had asked me then, which fortunately they did not, why I remained a Catholic, I might well have said that it was because I knew of no other place to go.

My spiritual depression at the time of the Council might have gone on much longer than it did, had I not gone to Puerto Rico, where I met a Capuchin friar who was as close to St. Francis as I think it is possible to be, at least in this world. During the years 1961 through 1964, I sometimes went to San Juan between school terms to serve as a public member of boards that were empowered to determine the minimum wage scales for industries involved in doing business between Puerto Rico and the United States mainland. It was, of course, because of my association with John Fogarty that I was given these appointments, and I was glad to serve since the function of the boards was to strengthen the island economy, as well as to make sure that workers were being paid a just wage.

The government provided board members with hotel space, but I had quickly seen that I would never learn anything about the lives of Puerto Rican workers while I lived in the world of Hilton hotels. Consequently, on my first assignment, I inquired around at the Department of Labor office and found out from one of the secretaries, who was a devout Catholic, that I might find what I was looking for on the Calle San Francisco at the monastery of the Capuchins.

These friars welcomed me as their guest in a monastic building that went back to Spanish times, and I was gratefully
able to stay there when I was working on the wage boards.
Indeed, as one priest among the guests put it, the monastery
was sort of a "clerical flop house" where one met a variety
of missionaries and others coming and going in and out of
Latin America. The food was simple; the talk was fascinating; the beds were hard; and the place was permeated with
kindness.

There I met a man whom I knew only as Padre Venard.
He not only wore the habit of St. Francis in the bitter barrio
called ironically La Perla, but he lived what that habit sig-
nified in those impoverished streets day and night. He
worked tirelessly to find jobs for the hundreds of unem-
ployed men of the barrio, displaced stevedores whose jobs
had been lost to mechanization; he stood up for them in the
sordid world of the night courts; he tried to restore family
life that was frequently uprooted when women found work
in light industries but men could not.

One night he invited me to go into the barrio where he
was to say Mass. At first, I hesitated because La Perla was
not a safe place for Yankees to walk at night, or so I had been
told in a government guidebook. But Padre Venard said,
"Don't worry for you will be with me. When I first went
down there, I was scared too because they threw things at
me and said they didn't want any priests around there. But
now it's O.K."

We made our way to a broken-down chapel in a narrow
street, which appeared to be deserted. Presently, however,
three or four boys in tattered clothes appeared and greeted
Venard with gusto.

"When is the Mass scheduled to begin?" I asked. He
smiled and said, "When the boys ring the bell and the
people show up."

After a bit the boys pulled on an old, frayed rope hanging down from the belfry and in about forty-five minutes the chapel was filled and Mass began.

Much of that night we spent going from cantina to cantina, and at each stop Venard pulled slips of paper from his habit pocket and distributed them to men. I jokingly accused him of running a numbers racket, but he said that on each of those slips there was an address where work might be found the next morning. That was what he called his employment service. Later we went to the night court where one or two of Venard's parishoners showed up after a brawl; he, of course, interceded for them and they were released in his custody, on the somewhat dubious promise that they would not be back any time soon.

I came and went, but that was Padre Venard's life in the streets of La Perla all the time. Often he came home exhausted and one might find him curled up asleep in his habit in any one of the remote corners of the old monastery. I have no idea what he thought about the doings in Rome during Vatican II. I suspect that he was too busy to give it much thought. But I saw him living in that Spirit who, faith teaches, is supposed to be the guide of Councils. Von Balthasar has rightly observed that saints are the best apology for the Faith because they demonstrate the gift of the Spirit, for Whom they have made room within souls swept clean of selfishness. I think Padre Venard was a saint, and I am certain that just being with him helped me to come out of the pointless, and essentially self-centered, depression that had come on me as a reaction to much about the Council and the real life of the Catholic Church that I had not begun to grasp.

Having long since studied the documents developed by Vatican II and in its immediate aftermath, I have gained what I hope is a properly informed idea of what the Council actually said and did with regard to such matters as liturgical reform, biblical scholarship, and ecclesiology. The documents are clear and obviously well-intentioned. The same, I think, cannot always be said for some who invoke the "spirit of Vatican II" to promote their various causes, including even such things as the so-called liturgies of "White Witches," a very medieval expression loaded with dire racist and sexist implications.

As the work of Vatican II brought with it many changes in the life of the Church, so 1965 brought a major change in my life, which was, quite probably, a response to what the Council had had to say about increasing the role of the laity. In an unprecedented action, the major administrative post of Vice President for Academic Affairs was offered to me at Providence College. I accepted this offer and immediately found myself becoming what the Dominican Provincial chose to describe as a "buffer state" between the hounds of heaven and an increasingly large group of lay faculty members, many of whom had ideas about the future of the college that were to be no less traumatic for the "Old Guard" than Vatican II itself.

NINE

When the Girls Came

I almost did not become Vice President for Academic Affairs at Providence College in 1965, for at the very time this position was offered to me, I had decided to move to another institution. Indeed during the time of my discontent with what I thought was going on at Vatican II, I had even been tempted by a position at the United States Office of Education in Washington, but one visit to that repository of forgotten statistics had convinced me that there must be better places to work.

My problem was really very simple. I was forty-nine; we had seven children; and I was a Professor at Providence College, where salaries for that rank were given a rating of D on the scale of the American Association of University Professors. Like many other laymen teaching in Catholic schools, I had to supplement my income. I did this by writing editorials for the diocesan newspaper and by what seemed like an endless round of talks and lectures. For example, in 1963–64, I gave a series of lectures on the British novel at a state-supported college; a lecture on ecumenism at Hampton–Sydney College in Virginia; and for six or more talks at Catholic colleges. That same year I spoke at an international Pax Romana meeting in Montreal, gave four lectures at a Christian Humanism Conference in North Carolina, a talk at Brown University, and numerous speeches at dinners, guilds, communion breakfasts, and high schools.

Much as I have always enjoyed talking, this was too much. I wanted to settle into a job to which I could afford to give the time and attention needed to do it really well. I saw no prospect of further advancement at Providence College where all major administrative positions were traditionally held by Dominicans. Thus I had agreed to accept the position of dean at a Catholic college in Florida, which had been offered to me at a substantial increase in salary, when I was astonished by a letter from Father Louis Every, the Dominican Provincial, that opened the way for me to remain at Providence as a Vice President. I requested, and was granted, a release from the Florida institution, accepted the promotion at Providence, and thus became involved in promoting an academic revolution there, which was, ironically, an example of the way in which many Catholic institutions responded to the very Council that I had earlier found it so difficult to accept. This might be taken as evidence that Divine Providence is not without a sense of humor.

The stage for the new era was set by the announcement that there would soon be a new president at the college. After Father Robert Slavin's death in 1961, a truly remarkable Dominican, Father Cyril Dore, had virtually come out of retirement to act as an interim president. He had been literally the first student when the college opened and had been assigned there as a faculty member after his ordination. He was well known in the Rhode Island Community, especially because of his concern for minority groups, and had served many years as Dean and Academic Vice President. He knew and believed that the college would have to undergo major changes in its administration and in its curriculum, which had not been much altered in forty years.

That immense task, however, was to be reserved for a

much younger Dominican, William Paul Haas, who was approaching his fortieth year. Bill Haas was a talented, many-sided, bright young man, whom I had met one summer when I was doing some teaching at the Dominican center in Dover, Massachusetts. He had a doctoral degree in philosophy from the University of Fribourg in Switzerland, an excellent grasp of contemporary thought, and had gained experience in the operation of American higher education at Notre Dame and Wabash College, where he had held an ecumenical teaching post.

Having been appointed as Academic Vice President under Father Dore, I began preparations for the coming of the new President in the fall of 1965. I spent most of the summer setting up a system of faculty personnel records, of which the college had virtually none. I also began the groundwork for a complete review of the curriculum, the academic departments, and the general degree requirements. My family lived at a rented beach house while I commuted about seventy miles daily going to the college in early morning and returning for the dinner hour. Meanwhile my wife and I were in the process of purchasing a rather handsome old house on Providence's historic East Side, not far from the site of my former parish. This house was to be the center of many social gatherings at which Bill Haas was to meet many leaders of the Providence community who were not Catholics. It was Mildred's role to be the hostess not only in her own home but also at various functions at the college.

That fall the new President swept in like the autumn wind and all sorts of dead leaves began to fly. He set up a staff organization with Vice Presidents, in addition to myself, for such things as business administration, development, and community relations. Business and financial affairs were the responsibility of another layman in the new administration, Joseph Byron, a former state purchasing agent and a close friend of John Fogarty, at whose office I had met Joe many times.

New office "complexes" to house the activities of these staff people sprang up. The President was flanked within his own such complex by the Development Vice President and myself. Typically of life at Catholic colleges, the renovated area we occupied in our very modern and tastefully appointed offices had been at various times a temporary location for St. Pius church, a science laboratory, and a study hall. Just before its renovation it had been used as a sewing room, with all the grace and charm of a deserted junk yard.

To attract and retain a professionally qualified number of new faculty was part of my responsibility. Most of them were to be laymen and not all of them were to be Catholics. The college itself had many non-Catholic students and drew heavily from public high schools; moreover it was understood that much-needed federal grants, especially in the sciences, required that they could be given to church-affiliated schools only if they did not discriminate in their hiring and admissions policies.

Moreover, the Dominicans simply did not have the qualified manpower to staff the academic departments, and they had finally realized, as the Jesuits knew from long experience, that keeping almost a hundred priests without salary in one institution was not the most efficient thing to do, especially when vocations were declining.

In order to obtain professionally qualified faculty and make the college truly competitive in the academic marketplace, we needed not only much improved salaries but also the usual basic structures for participatory academic government. Colleges and universities could not operate as seminaries and houses of study had done under virtual one-man rule. Indeed, as an administrator I chose to continue to teach at least one course in order to give emphasis to the idea that in college academic government faculty shared with administrators, who need not necessarily be their natural enemies. The collegial concept had roots, in fact, in many ancient universities, as was the case with the senate at Fribourg.

Among my very first goals were to obtain faculty participation in creating a Senate, a Committee on Rank and Tenure, and the writing of a Faculty Manual that would spell out faculty rights and responsibilities. With all this to do, I had no longer the time, and happily not the need, to go about giving talks and lectures.

At Providence, as was the case at some other Catholic colleges, we found that no new structures or policies could be put in place and given proper legal status until central control by the President could be dismantled. It was, first of all, necessary to resuscitate the legal governing board, called the Corporation, which had been moribund for many years. That was the only body which had full legal authority under the college charter from Rhode Island to carry out the basic things that needed to be done. Indeed, they were so basic that Bill Haas used to say to me that sometimes he felt that he and I were really the Founding Fathers of the institution.

It was his job to bring the Corporation back to life, and he went about it with customary gusto. He also created a presidential Advisory Board, made up of leading financial figures drawn from the general community and not exclusively from Catholic circles. This group was to help in implementing a Ten Year Development Plan, an immediate and vital aspect of which was the construction of a library building. The college library had its very limited collection housed on the third floor of Harkins Hall, a building which contained administrative offices, classrooms, the residence of most of the Dominican community, a cafeteria, a book store, and a gymnasium that doubled as an auditorium.

With the Corporation reformed and strengthened by some competent laymen, together with the Bishop, the controlling majority of Dominicans, and the Provincial as Chairman, Bill Haas' administration began to move forward. After endless committee meetings, which were often as boring to attend as they would be to relate, the new Faculty Senate was duly elected and held its very first meeting on January 31, 1968. By May of that same year, a new Committee on Rank and Tenure, over which it was my often painful duty to preside, had disposed of 61 cases of tenure, promotion, or new appointments. It came to be known among the faculty as the RAT Committee and I had to direct its destiny for the next fourteen years.

Of course, the time when many changes were taking place at Providence College under Bill Haas were also times of general unrest on college campuses, for the protests were mounting against the war in Vietnam. Since Providence also experienced the student discontent, I who had once been a student activist at Columbia, now found myself on the other side of the desk as an administrator who was frequently called upon to deal with young men who wanted to tear down the Establishment but were somewhat vague as to what ought to take its place.

There was some disruption of academic life in the college during the period of 1969–70, but there was not a student revolution, thanks to the wise policies of Bill Haas, a very understanding Commanding Officer of the college R.O.T.C., and the development of elements of student participatory government.

But by September of 1971 two very revolutionary steps had been taken by the college administration and the governing Corporation, with the complete support of the Faculty Senate. The first was the removal of what had been a general degree requirement of five courses in what was largely Aristotelian philosophy and five courses for all Catholic students in what had once been called theology but had become religious studies. Both subjects were taken up into the structure of a new team-taught two-year sequential course for all freshmen and sophomores called Development of Western Civilization. This was called "creeping secularism" by its conservative opponents and it was said that I was largely responsible.

The second revolutionary action which was implemented in the fall of 1971 was so revolutionary as to create severe traumas among some Dominicans and a number of older alumni. Women were admitted to the student body and, of course, to the faculty. But all through the struggles to win approval for these truly startling innovations, in which I had to play a leading role, I always had the support of two stalwart key Dominicans, both of whom understood the real world and the developing Church: Mark Heath, the Chairman of Religious Studies, and Thomas Peterson, the Dean of the college, who later succeeded Bill Haas as President.

The reasons for the admission of women to the previously all male student body at Providence College were not ideological, although many who supported the change believed in the concept of co-education. As was the case with many small liberal arts colleges co-education came to Providence College because without it the institution might well have disappeared. Undergraduate enrollment had peaked at 2703 in 1966–67, when tuition was $1000 per year. By 1969–70 it had risen to $1700 and by the fall of 1970 enrollment fell to 2109. Meanwhile, following a national trend, enrollment in public institutions was rising.

It was evident that Providence College, which depended almost totally on tuition for its income, could not survive effectively without a substantial increase in its enrollment. It was also evident from a sophisticated study done at Princeton that the best students in secondary schools were simply not interested in going to single-sex colleges. The Director of Admissions at Princeton said as much and gave little credence to what he called "ancient arguments to defend monastic life at Princeton."

Our own studies and experience, together with the facts about falling enrollments, convinced the college corporation to approve a policy of admitting women students and of taking all the necessary planning and hiring steps to make this policy functional by September, 1971.

The way to that goal was not easy, for its opponents summoned up all the "ancient arguments to defend the monastic life" at Providence, even as they had done at Princeton. Some of these arguments are interesting because they reveal much deeper issues in the life of the Church that are still by no means resolved:

1. Women come to co-educational schools to find husbands, and are not seriously motivated as students;

2. Providence was founded to help poor Catholic young men to achieve leadership positions in society; women do not play such leadership roles, and their admission would reduce the number of places available to poor local young men who might someday become civic leaders;

3. Women college students tend to be militant feminists; they would be unwelcome agitators;

4. Co-education always presents a moral danger; illicit sexual activity would increase because of it;

5. Too many changes are taking place in the Church; Providence should remain a firm, traditional, all-male place of solid Thomistic educational stability;

6. Alumni loyalty would diminish if there were female students, faculty, and administrators on campus, for this

would obscure the healthy masculine image projected by the Dominicans;

7. The presence of women in classes would create a certain "playground" atmosphere; men prefer male company when they are engaged in serious work.

Even some who reluctantly supported the new policy for economic reasons felt impelled to issue dire warnings. Indeed one member of the Dominican community who belonged to this group produced a printed pamphlet, which had the title *When the Girls Come*, and offered all sorts of advice to male students in anticipation of the female onslaught.

This document, which has some historic value, was a gold mine of macho mythology. "What woman," it asked, "isn't looking for a man? A co-ed would rather be the light of some man's life than nobody's *cum laude* scholar."

Moreover, the learned clerical author averred, "Woman's brain is conditioned by the womb." Aristotle could not have put it more aptly. As for women on the faculty, readers were told that, "Studies indicate that identical material presented by a woman has less authority than it has when presented by a man." Students were further informed that, "The male student, reared in a masculine culture, often chafes under the authority of a woman teacher, and even resents taking assignments from her."

One of the most notable statements made in this extraordinary document was, "The effect a woman has on a man is different from the effect she has on a woman." Male students must realize that, "...man still stands in awe of woman's biological function.... Because he senses, with rare masculine insight, that she is the hub of the human universe.... In fact, man is afraid of woman."

Evidently this must have been true of at least one man at Providence College, but when 331 young women arrived among the freshman class of 869 in the fall of 1971, none of the male students seemed the least bit frightened. Incidentally, administrators were a lot less frightened about the future when that figure of 869 was contrasted with the previous year's all-male freshman class of 549. Nor were faculty members frightened when they learned that the new class was made up of students thirty-six percent of whom were in the top fifth of their secondary school classes, as contrasted with only 26 percent in the all-male class of the previous year.

Some observers of the campus scene who had worked long and hard on the committees involved in preparing to receive the women students were heard to say that 1971 was the year when Western Civilization and women came to the campus for the first time. And they meant it to mean what it seemed to mean: the women were truly a force for a much more civilized campus.

All in all, then, things were looking up at Providence in the autumn of 1971, although we had lost Bill Haas as President. He had resigned his office late in the previous spring. Later he was laicized at his own request, married, and went on to a very successful career in secular higher education. His successor was my good friend and supporter in all my "revolutionary" efforts on behalf of women and Western Civilization, Thomas Peterson, a Dominican who well understood and had carefully studied what higher education for Catholics must become in the post-Conciliar period.

The five years I worked with Bill Haas were years when Providence College really came of age. There was a fine new library that won national architectural awards; there was a faculty of 176 men and women, 74 of whom had the earned doctorate and all of whom were professionally structured and responsibly participant in academic government. There was a modernized academic physical plant; there had been total curriculum up-dating; and there was full co-education. Totally new departments of Psychology and Art had been created, together with all manner of student services and a whole new financial and fund-raising structure.

Bill Haas, like hundreds of others, chose to leave the priesthood, but he left behind a very important part of himself at Providence College. He spent that time for the good of others, and it will bring them endless returns in their lives. I stated to the Corporation that I had found it "a wonderfully tiring experience to serve as Academic Vice President under William Paul Haas, O.P." In the perspective of time, I do not find that to be a statement I would care to alter.

The rest of the time that I was Academic Vice President was not quite so revolutionary as was the time when the girls came. It was a time of steady development, and Providence College is today generally rated among the better private liberal arts colleges in the United States. It is surely one more piece of evidence that such Catholic colleges are viable in the Church and in America's pluralistic culture.

There is, indeed, a real need for such institutions if American pluralism is to endure in the face of homogenized state-controlled universities and colleges. Certainly, there is no place for the kind of mere indoctrination which tries to package religion so neatly as to miss utterly the mystery of the grandeur of God revealed in Christ. But there is surely a place for colleges that pursue the wisdom of Catholicism, as distinguished from the current varieties of Epicurean, Cynic, or Luddite behavior that are offered to the young in our times.

And, wherever possible, there should be opportunities offered to American students, especially those of Catholic background, to have both a living and a learning experience of the old Catholic cultures of Europe. Bill Haas understood this well because of his association with Fribourg and sug-

gested to me in 1967 that I might go there in the summer of
that year to explore the possibility of having some of our
undergraduates in an existing junior year program actually
enroll in courses offered to regularly enrolled students at Fribourg, instead of being limited to courses offered by the
American program then in place.

The upshot of this had been that Mildred and I had had an
opportunity to travel not only to Fribourg but to other places
where American students were spending their junior years
abroad. We visited the University of Madrid, for example,
and an American program in Rome. And I had a meeting
with the head of the English seminar at Freiburg in Germany. We were then not only engaged in such professional
matters but we were also two middle-aged people still in
love and having a sort of delayed honeymoon. It was also
the beginning of our love affair with Italy.

That summer of 1967 was our first visit to Rome and I
shall never forget the sense of exaltation I felt as we looked
up at the interior of the great dome of St. Peter's and saw
inscribed there the words which had always meant so much
to me, even in my Anglican days, for the Latin read: *Tu es
Petrus et supra hanc petram aedificabo ecclesiam meam*
(Mt.16:18). Of course, I had not the faintest inkling then
that more than twenty years later I would walk under that
dome on my way to say Mass in the San Clemente chapel.

It was 1980 before we went to Italy again in connection
with Providence College's programs of study abroad. This
time we travelled with Father Ambrose McAlister, a fine Dominican sculptor and teacher from the college's Art Department, and a group of about twenty-five of his students, both
men and women. Journeying from London across the channel to Paris and down into the Toulouse area, we proceeded
at length to Pietrasanta on the Mediterranean near Carrara
in the marble country, about an hour away from Florence.

There we stayed all through July for a program of studies

in which the students did courses in art history and in studio art. I had the great joy of teaching a small group a course that dealt with Shelley, Byron, and the Pisan circle, and was able to lead students to the actual sites of some of their poetry, as well as to Viareggio, where a memorial Piazza P.B. Shelley commemorates the tragic drowning of the poet off the coast of that city.

It was in Pietrasanta that I learned a lesson about politics in Italy which I often think of when then conversation turns to the so-called liberation theology. The government of the town was in the hands of the local Communist Party and I came to know one of its ardent members, who was also a man of both business and property. One night over a glass of wine, I asked him if he really wanted Italy to become a Communist nation. He just laughed and said, "Whenever Italy becomes Communist, Communism in Italy will be finished." And he drew his hand across his throat as if to suggest it would be cut.

A student who was with our group that summer and who is now settled in an academic career once wrote to me to say how much all of the students had learned living and learning in Pietrasanta. He called it an "enchanted summer" in their lives. And I know that the women students all heartily agreed.

The following summer was, in a very different sense, a truly "enchanted" time for both Mildred and myself. It was in the spring of that year that we had learned that it had suddenly become possible for me to be ordained as a Roman Catholic priest.

If anyone had suggested such a thing to me when I first went to Providence College in 1949, I would have said that it was impossible. But then if someone had told me that women would someday be students and teachers at the college, I would have said that was also impossible—about as impossible as the Mass ever being said in English.

TEN

Where St. Brendan Discovered America

Bishop Thomas C. Kelly, O.P., now the Archbishop of Louisville, graduated from Providence College in the Class of 1953 and I recalled him as a student in one of my English classes. Thus I was delighted to see him in the role of General Secretary of the National Conference of Catholic Bishops appearing on a TV news program late in the spring of 1981. But I was utterly astonished by what he was saying, which was that under a Pastoral Provision approved by the Pope it would now be possible for married Episcopal priests who became Catholics to qualify and be ordained as priests in the Roman Catholic Church.

My first reaction was to say to Mildred that if this was true, it was clear evidence that even the Pope was capable of making serious mistakes when it came to administrative decisions.

I was even more convinced of this when I read in *Time* magazine that some clergy were leaving the Episcopal Church to become Catholics because the Episcopalians were ordaining priestesses. If this was so, it struck me as a rather negative, and therefore questionable, reason for becoming a

Catholic. I could think of some better ones, such as the belief that the Catholic Church is the Church founded by Christ and continuously present in the world doing His work ever since the Apostolic Age. Since Pope Leo XIII, as the Vicar of Christ, had said that Episcopalian ordinations were null and void, it hardly mattered if they were conferred upon women.

In any case, I concluded that the Pastoral Provision probably had nothing to do with my situation. From what I could gather from news reports it came about as the result of a petition submitted to Rome through the Bishops of the United States on behalf of some Episcopalians, both clerical and lay, who were displeased with recent developments in their Church and were seeking what was described as "full communion" with the Catholic Church. It was, as I understood it, limited in its application to the United States. I presumed it was also limited to persons in circumstances similar to the individuals who had first sought "full communion" according to very specific terms. I thought, for example, that it applied only to Episcopal priests currently active in their ministry but who now wished to become Catholics.

The full facts regarding the origins of the Pastoral Provision are not known to me. No doubt they will be set forth at some future date by American church historians. This has not yet been done in any scholarly depth, but when it is there will no doubt be a prominent role given to the Reverend James Parker, who was the first man ordained under the Pastoral Provision. Prior to his ordination Father Parker had served in the Episcopalian ministry for twenty-five years and, as a convert, was appointed to assist the then Bishop Bernard Law of Springfield-Cape Girardeau, whom the Holy See named to be the Ecclesiastical Delegate in the matter of the Pastoral Provision. Bishop Law has, of course, become widely known and respected as the very able Cardinal Archbishop of Boston.

At the time it was announced, my lack of knowledge about the Pastoral Provision was equalled only by my lack of knowledge of what was currently happening to whatever was left of the Anglo-Catholic faction in the Episcopal Church. I had had literally no contact with its fortunes since 1949.

I was, therefore, completely in the dark when I read news accounts of how the Pastoral Provision might apply to Episcopalians who became Catholics but wished to "retain a common identity," which sounded to me as if what they wanted was an exclusive club within the Church. Upon investigation, however, I discovered that this was not quite the case. Those who longed for "a common identity" comprised a unique group of seventeen former Episcopalian priests and some twelve hundred lay persons, who appeared to live mostly in Texas and California. Having separated themselves from the Episcopal Church, these individuals had formed, several years earlier than 1981, what they chose to describe as the Pro-Diocese of St. Augustine of Canterbury under the guidance of an elderly Anglo-Catholic priest, Father Albert Dubois, who had subsequently died.

I recalled meeting Albert Dubois in England in 1948. At that time he was talking about the possibility of an "Anglican Rite" within the Catholic Church made up initially of former Anglicans, who would be given their own canonical status under the Pope, with their own hierarchy and a liturgy that would preserve something called the Anglican liturgical tradition, whatever that might be. Something of that sort of thing seemed to be back of the creation of the Pro-Diocese of St. Augustine in the far reaches of California and Texas. I remember asking Gordon Wadhams about this on the last occasion I was with him before his death. He simply shook his head and remarked, "They do not wish to belong to the Episcopal Church and they are not in the Catholic

Church. No one seems to know to what Church they do belong."

According to a position paper submitted to Bishop Law after his appointment as Ecclesiastical Delegate, the seventeen clergymen and twelve hundred lay persons of the Pro-Diocese of St. Augustine of Canterbury did want to belong to the Catholic Church but preferred to be allowed to keep a "common identity" within it. Among other things, they wanted a liturgy that would, of all things, reflect the so-called Sarum Use, so beloved by Percy Dearmer and so generally scorned among pro-Roman Anglo-Catholics. They also wanted to use the vernacular of Cranmer's time rather than that of modern revisions of the English *Prayer Book*. They hoped to have a special calendar that would include some local English saints, although no specific mention was made of "Blessed Charles, King and Martyr." And they hoped that other Catholics might learn to appreciate Anglican church music.

All of this seemed quite harmless, if a bit arcane. The same position paper, however, contained a suggestion that was, perhaps, more serious in nature. It was suggested that there might well be erected a personal prelature, or even a diocese, just for them, but "in fullest unity with the Holy See." The supposed benefit of this would be to preserve "common identity" by not scattering them among the rest of their fellow Catholics and preventing what they regarded as the danger of "total absorption."

That seemed to me to be a bit of asking to have one's cake and eating it too. But I recalled what Newman wrote in 1850, "It is no work of a day to convince the intellect of an Englishman that Catholicism is true. And even when the intellect is convinced, a thousand subtle influences interpose in arrest of what should follow." What should follow, one might suppose, would be to seek membership in the Catho-

174 · *Where St. Brendan Discovered America*

lic Church unconditionally. Evidently, it seemed, the new Pastoral Provision was offering some different alternatives, at least as possibilities.

Apart from this question of a "common identity," I wondered about the impact of the Pastoral Provision upon American Catholics. There would be the predictable reaction of *National Catholic Reporter* types who would object to having to put up with "right wing" former Episcopalians. Angry feminists would denounce the male chauvinists whom they would certainly perceive as being in flight from the newly ordained Episcopal priestesses. Those who wanted to make marriage an option for the clergy would see this as a step in the right direction, but would object that it was unfair to Catholic priests who were not able to exercise the priesthood because they had married. Those who opposed any relaxation of the discipline of clerical celibacy would see a sinister plot to undermine the celibate ideal. Enthusiastic promoters of reunion-all-around versions of ecumenism would deplore the ordination of former Episcopal priests as harmful to the cause of mutual love and understanding between Catholics and Episcopalians, especially because it would call attention to the fact that Rome has declared Anglican ordinations to be null and void.

That there would be a large number of conversions, with the people and the priests of whole Episcopalian parishes all coming into the Catholic Church, may also have been in the minds of some Catholics. I later gained the impression that there may even have been expectations of that sort in Rome. I had no such illusions, for I knew from hard experience that while Anglo-Catholic minority groups always talk a lot about "going to Rome" whenever the Episcopal Church acts according to its Protestant character, very few ever want to pay the price of taking the trip.

I certainly did wonder if the cost of maintaining married

priests had been fully appreciated when the Pastoral Provision was planned. Having lived as a lay Catholic for over thirty years, and having raised a family of seven children, I found it difficult to imagine how my wife and I could have done so on the very small salaries commonly paid to priests. How would the problems of housing have been solved? Would our domestic tribe have shared some great barn of a rectory with a celibate pastor and his assistant, if he had an assistant? Had anyone calculated the amount of time and energy which conscientious Catholic fathers might be expected to give to their domestic responsibilities and how this might limit the time that a married priest might have to give to parochial work?

In the face of such practical difficulties, it had always seemed to me during my years as a Catholic that the policy of clerical celibacy was a sensible one for the Church to follow, especially in view of the apparent reluctance of most Catholics to contribute as generously to the Church as their Protestant neighbors did to their respective denominations. People who habitually put fifty cents or a dollar in the collection basket whenever they went to Mass over a period of many years could not reasonably be expected to support a growing clerical family, to say nothing of paying for its health plan and pension benefits.

On a less practical level, I knew, of course, that there were married priests in the Church's Oriental rites and that before Canon 33 of the Council of Elvira in 306 there was probably no canonical enforcement of celibacy for priests in the Latin West. The legal position of the Orthodox is that priests and deacons may marry before ordination but that bishops must be celibate. And there seems to be some evidence that such a system of discipline was developing in the West before the fourth century.

Furthermore, I was aware that prior to the 1917 Code of

Canon Law there had been legislation permitting a married man to be ordained a priest, provided that his wife freely entered a religious community. I also knew that under the 1917 Code the impediment of marriage could be dispensed by the Holy See and that Pius XII had granted permission for the ordination of certain German Lutheran ministers who became Catholics during the course of his pontificate.

Thus in spite of all my misgivings, I was most curious to know whether or not the Pastoral Provision was in any way applicable to a man like myself—a former Episcopal priest who was married, with children and grandchildren, and who had been a convert for almost half of his sixty-four years.

I, therefore, decided to call Bishop Thomas Kelly, my former student, and ask him. He seemed very pleased to hear from me and said that he thought I would certainly be eligible to seek ordination under the Pastoral Provision and that he hoped I would write to Bishop Bernard Law for further information.

It took some time, but I finally concluded that Mildred and various friends who were urging me to make such a written inquiry were right. I was especially influenced by the opinion of Father Tom Peterson, who had become President of Providence College. He reminded me that he had often expressed the opinion that the time would come when I could be ordained as a Catholic priest. Indeed when I had given Providence College the chalice I had used as a military chaplain, he had accepted it as a "loan" and had told me he thought I would ask to have it back some day. I knew that he had used that chalice himself at Masses which he had offered for the intention of my future ordination. It was, he said, his belief that my vocation in the Episcopal Church had been a real vocation and that my being unable to fulfill it in the Catholic Church made it no less real. Now, he said, the obstacle to my doing so might possibly be removed and I was bound in conscience to inquire about that possibility.

Not finding myself able to rationalize things any further, I finally wrote to Bishop Law on July 29, 1981, after having discussed the matter informally with Bishop Louis Gelineau, who had succeeded Bishop McVinney some time before. Bishop Gelineau, with whom I was acquainted, had been encouraging, and I had told him that if it should prove possible for me to become a priest, I would wish to do so.

This wish was something I had felt many times but had never discussed with anyone other than Mildred. Having once believed that, as an Episcopal priest, I was offering the Eucharist, I felt a sense of deprivation in not ever being able to do so in the reality of my life as a Catholic. I felt that Bishop Law would understand this and I told him of it in my letter.

His very prompt and gracious response contained the following:

> My understanding of the Pastoral Provision is that it would indeed cover someone under your circumstances. Consequently, it is perfectly in order for you to proceed with your application through the Bishop of Providence. Bishop Gelineau would then submit the dossier to me when it is completed.
>
> I can readily understand what a tremendous consolation it would be to you personally to be able to celebrate the Eucharistic Sacrifice.

This letter concluded with Bishop Law's assurance of his willingness to be of any possible help. I felt already greatly helped by his response, especially to that part of my letter in which I had said the following:

> I am sure that you can appreciate the fact that at my age it would be a great consolation to be able to offer the Sacrifice

of the Mass. While I am mindful of the parable of the workers in the vineyard, I may, perhaps, be pardoned for feeling that if the Catholic priesthood is to be open to married Episcopal priests who are becoming Catholics, it might also be open to those of us who came to the Church before that was possible.

I forwarded a copy of Bishop Law's letter to Bishop Gelineau, who responded promptly that he would seek further information regarding the process by which it would be necessary for him to proceed. On September 16 I had an interview with the Bishop during the course of which I made it clear that if I were to be ordained for the Diocese of Providence, I would assume complete responsibility not only for all my personal finances but also for the support of my wife in the event of my death. I was, of course, able to give such assurances because of my position at Providence College and my participation in its excellent health insurance and pension programs. Thus the economic problems that are normally associated with diocesan responsibilty for clergy in no way applied to my case; moreover, the Bishop would not need to be concerned in any way with the financial needs of my family.

Obviously, my whole situation was radically different from that of those who would ordinarily be coming into the Catholic priesthood under the Pastoral Provision, some of whom had young children. All of our children were independent adults. Moreover, unlike these new converts, my wife and I were very well known to the Catholic community and very familiar with the experience of living as lay people in the Church. Moreover, as a consequence of my teaching in the Western Civilization course at Providence College, I had been in constant touch with the literature of academic disciplines such as Church history, Biblical studies, and Development of Christian Thought. I had, after all, studied the liturgy with German Benedictines and much of Thomas Aquinas in my graduate work. I did not think that I would be found lacking in any of these subjects. My weak spots would be canon law and the more recent developments in moral theology, some of which had weaknesses of their own.

Moreover, my book on the history, organization, and doctrine of the Church had been personally commended in a letter sent to me by Pope Paul VI at the time when he was Archbishop of Milan and I had strong letters of support and recommendation from Dominican sources. Indeed I even had the assurance of any instruction I might require in liturgy, canon law, and moral theology from Dominicans who were professional teachers of those subjects.

My greatest help, however, came from Monsignor William Varsanyi, a long-time friend, an expert canonist, and Bishop Gelineau's Vicar for Canonical Affairs. The process for those seeking ordination under the Pastoral Provision was, quite properly, both long and thorough. Bill Varsanyi guided me through the preparation of the complex dossier that would eventually have to go to Rome, and I was to be told in 1984 by a very reliable Roman authority that this dossier was, as he put it, "perfect." Had it not been for Bill's expert help, it would certainly never have deserved such an appraisal.

This dossier had to contain, in addition to records of baptism, marriage, and family histories, evidence of the stability of our marriage and of my wife's consent to my seeking ordination. Another important entry was the complete record of my ordination in the Episcopal Church, which contained evidence that Bishop Washburn, who had ordained me, had himself been made an Episcopalian bishop in a line of succession which included none other than Bishop de Landsbergher et de Roche of the Old Catholic See of Utrecht.

Three sets of the dossier were sent to Bishop Law by

Bishop Gelineau with a very fine covering letter. The appropriate copies were then forwarded to the Congregation for the Doctrine of the Faith late in November of 1981. Nothing was heard about it until March of 1983. I had not expected Rome to be anything but slow in responding to my petition. Had it proved to be otherwise, I would have been disappointed. Having been a Catholic and an administrator in a Catholic college for many years, I knew that any genuinely Roman decision would take a long time. Meanwhile there would be an assessment process to go through in Washington, and if all went well, qualifying examinations, both oral and written, that would have to be completed in due time.

Although I continued as a member of the faculty at Providence College, I decided to leave the office of Vice President and did so in May of 1982. I also took a sabbatical leave of one semester because Mildred and I had decided that while we, in a sense, waited for Rome to come to us with some word about my petition, we should go to Rome and a lot of other places both in Italy and Greece.

Our Italian sojourn began with a visit to Rome late in May, and we found ourselves one Sunday quite by chance at a Papal Mass in St. Peter's not very far from the Holy Father but not close enough for me to ask him about the progress of my petition.

We drove down to the beautiful tourist traps at Sorrento and Capri; visited the ancient site of the Greek colony at Paestum; and drove on to Gallipoli, another ancient Greek city, which is not to be confused with the famous place in Turkey where the Australians suffered such heavy losses in the First World War. Our Gallipoli is on the Ionian Sea and was, among other things, the port from which the legions of Rome sailed for the conquest of Jerusalem in 70 A.D. We lived in an apartment right on the ancient harbor and I

sometimes imagined the sound of those great legions coming up to our windows at night when what I was actually
hearing was just some rather noisy local fishermen, one of
whom had the old Roman name of Claudio.

With Gallipoli as our base, we visited much of the Adriatic
coastal area, including such places as Bari, Brindisi, and the
Gargano peninsula. Each day began for us in a way which
seemed highly eccentric to the local police, who kept a very
friendly eye on our extended visit. What was strange to
them was that we went down the main street to Mass, and
in the church itself I proved to be something of a sensation as
the only male worshipper in the congregation of elderly
women.

But in that ancient city we had occasion to be reminded of
how deep in its past were the roots of that religious regard
for the rites of the dead which survives even in the midst of
events that are highly contemporary. The day Italy won the
European soccer championship by beating the Germans in
1982 we stood on the balcony of our apartment and shared
in the bedlam of cheering and celebration, as we joined in
shouting "Italia, Numero Uno."

Suddenly, however, total silence swept over the cele-
brants as a funeral procession approached and went
through. Only when it had left that section of the city did the
celebration resume with even more vigorous shouting that
was all the more so because the victory had been over the
very unpopular Germans.

We made many friends in Gallipoli, where a former colleague at Providence had returned home to retire, and we
spent many pleasant hours with him and those to whom he
introduced us. We left for Greece early in September and
returned to Providence near the end of October, after having
stayed part of the time on Crete. Everywhere we were impressed by the evident devotion of many Greek Orthodox

men and women to the Mother of God and we were struck by the fact that Holy Liturgy celebrated in Greek Orthodox churches leaves no doubt that here the Mystical Body of Christ worships in such a way as to express its sense of the beauty of holiness and the transcendent glory of God. Such adoration intensifies the sense of communion not only with those present but with the Church Triumphant in heaven.

Perhaps we were especially edified by the Greek Liturgy because it stood in such perfect contrast to so much that is painfully familiar in so many Catholic churches in the United States. These places, built to resemble vast milk barns in their circular form, present the Eucharist as if it were a pleasant parish picnic meal, presided over by genial clerics, in a few instances actually dressed as clowns, to the sound of folksy guitars. One finds it hard to conceive that what is really going on is meant to be in some sense the worship that the Church offers to God as His due.

Our somewhat reluctant return to the American scene late in the year disclosed that there was still no news about my petition. After the Christmas recess, I returned to teaching at Providence College and prepared myself systematically for the oral examinations I was to take in Washington.

After Bishop Gelineau was informed in March that my petition had been approved in Rome, I knew that upon successful completion of all my qualifying examinations, the date for my ordination could be set. I also knew that once I had been ordained, I could not marry again, in the very unlikely event that an occasion to do so should arise if my wife were to die. The point is, of course, that while it is possible for a married man to become a priest, it is not possible for a Roman Catholic priest to marry and continue to function as a priest.

Moreover, I learned that after ordination I would be permitted to assist in a parish in the full range of priestly duties but that I would not be permitted to be a pastor or an associate pastor having what is called the ordinary "care of souls." Like most of the men ordained under the Pastoral Provision, I would probably be assigned to administrative, social, or educational work. In my case, this meant that I would be assigned to continue to teach at Providence College and that I might be given some part-time pastoral work. Another limitation on my exercise of the ministry would be that I could not do priestly work outside of the United States without special approval by the Holy See.

Some of these restrictions did not apply to men who were ordained to serve the very few scattered "common identity" parishes, for they could serve those parishes as their pastors. As things turned out, they also were to have approval for a liturgy described as an "Anglican Use" that would be permitted only in the "common identity" parishes; there was no Anglican Rite.

I heartily endorsed Rome's decision not to permit married priests ordained under the Pastoral Provision in full-time parochial assignments. No one then knew how parishes would react to married clergy or how the many practical problems associated with them could be managed. Furthermore, virtually all of those who were being ordained under the Pastoral Provision, as well as their wives, had no experience whatever of living as lay people in the Catholic Church. It would seem reasonable to think that one has to have some personal knowledge of what it is like to live as a Catholic before attempting to minister to Catholics as one of their parish priests.

What is more, Catholic bishops had had no experience of dealing with married priests and their wives. In this circumstance Bishop Law had requested a sympathetic Episcopalian bishop to prepare a brief paper that Catholic bishops might use in helping them to deal with the Pastoral Provision clerical families if they were to have any such in their dioceses. This paper wisely pointed out that Catholic bishops ought to realize that they might well have to be "more concerned with the wife than the priest." Wives of priests in the Catholic Church, he pointed out, would inevitably experience some sense of isolation; they would be helped by having a wise spiritual director. They might also be aided by being given an opportunity for orientation regarding what might be described as "the ethos and organization" of the Church. What was suggested was that Catholic bishops who dealt with Pastoral Provision clerical families ought to be prepared to give them a good deal of tender, loving care, especially in the initial stages of their new life.

I am inclined to suspect that all this advice from the Episcopalian bishop has not been widely used, but I have no way of knowing that. I can only say that he most certainly knew what he was talking about, especially with regard to recently married wives who themselves had come from religious backgrounds far removed from that of Anglo-Catholics. For a young woman raised, for example, as a Southern Baptist and recently married to an Anglo-Catholic clergyman, the Episcopal Church would certainly be a radically different environment. For such a person then to enter the world of Roman Catholicism as the wife of a priest would inevitably be truly traumatic. It might even prove to be a disaster.

All in all, the restrictions placed on the assignments of Pastoral Provision priests seemed to me to make a great deal of sense, but more attention to the special problems of their wives might conceivably have been forthcoming if the matters raised in the Episcopalian bishop's paper had been given greater consideration on the local level.

Having completed the final written examinations over a couple of days at the Chancery in May, I was delighted to learn from Jim Parker at the end of June that these written examinations had been evaluated by the members of the examining board and that I had passed all of them "with distinction." It had all been somewhat like going through the doctoral examinations all over again, and I had a similar sense of relief that the process was over.

This completed all the preparations for my ordination which had been required by the Holy See, and the date for my becoming a priest was set for August 27, with my ordination to the diaconate set three days earlier. I was especially pleased that August 27 was the feast of St. Monica, the mother of St. Augustine, for her persistent prayers had won his conversion and I hoped they would help me too. Both Mildred and I liked the name of Monica and had given it to be one of our daughters, who, rather like her namesake, turned out to be a very forthright young woman who would not take "No" for an answer.

I made an ordination retreat at a Benedictine priory and was greatly pleased upon returning from it to learn that among those who planned to be present for the ceremony were my old friends from World War II days, Father Charles Eggert and Archbishop Joseph Ryan. Bishop Gelineau invited Mildred and me to dinner at his residence the night before my ordination as a priest, and although she was the only woman among the guests, Mildred seemed right at home, for she had had similar experiences years before in the rectory at St. Stephen's.

The day of my ordination was a perfectly beautiful one and the setting in the Cathedral of Saints Peter and Paul was, like the music, magnificent. The Bishop and the cathedral clergy had done everything possible to make the occasion truly memorable, even to having it completely televised. In the sanctuary, with Bishop Gelineau as principal celebrant, were his Auxiliary Bishop and three Archbishops, including Joe Ryan. There were also over forty priests, including not only Charlie Eggert but also Joe Jurasko, who had received us into the Church in 1949.

In the congregation of more than five hundred sat an old friend, John Higgins, the retired Episcopalian Bishop of Rhode Island, who had written me a very kind note in response to his invitation. He suggested that my future might possibly hold even greater things for me, for Newman had been created a Cardinal at seventy-eight, while I was a mere sixty-six.

During the course of his remarks at the end of the Mass, Bishop Gelineau observed that when he had been asked what was now to become of Mildred, he had replied. "She's part of the package. She comes with Paul, and we're delighted by the opportunity to have Paul with us." As matters turned out, however, it was not to be quite that simple. The "package" concept was far more easily conceived than it could be implemented.

At any rate, Mildred and I were very fortunate to have our own home, an old colonial house, parts of which went back to 1745, in Kingston, Rhode Island, from which I continued to drive to Providence College, as I had been doing for some years. In various newspaper articles and on a television show, Mildred spoke of her role as that of Martha in the New Testament. She supported me, as she had always done, in all my work, especially in regard to typing my correspondence, my writing, and my teaching lectures.

At first I said Mass each morning at the convent of Sisters of the Cross and Passion, whose chaplain had recently died. Mildred accompanied me and we had many happy times after Mass with the Sisters, who always invited us to breakfast. In September, however, I was asked to meet with the pastor of St. Mary's, Newport, which is the oldest Catholic parish in Rhode Island, traditionally Irish in character, and the scene of the wedding of John F. Kennedy. The Auxiliary

Bishop, Kenneth Angell, had served there as an Assistant together with Father George Brendan McCarthy, who had become the pastor. It was Bishop Angell who told me that Father McCarthy was looking for some help on weekends and that he had consented to interview me.

Father McCarthy, I rapidly discovered, was one of those known in some clerical circles as a member of the F.B.I, which stands for "Foreign Born Irish." As I later came to know him, he seemed rather like a Marine Corps Master Gunnery Sergeant, which was a high compliment indeed, for it meant that he knew his business as a priest, did his job, and put up with no nonsense. He was not only an Irishman, but perhaps even more importantly, he came from County Kerry, where, according to one legend, St. Patrick never arrived because someone in Cork stole his donkey. It is, consequently, a most wonderfully mysterious place where the influence of the ancient Druids may be experienced even to this day in the very atmosphere of the lovely countryside and particularly beside the sea on the long stretches of strand.

The day he interviewed me, the pastor of St. Mary's sat firmly beneath a large portrait of Bishop McVinney which hung in a prominent place in the main parlor, not far from the portrait of the present Ordinary, which hung in the corridor. The tone of the interview might have been strained, for Father George, as he was known in the parish, was actually very nervous about having a married priest come to St. Mary's, even if it was to be just for a weekend Mass. He was, of course, taking a chance which others might not have dared to take, for no one had any idea of how the people were going to react or what might be involved. As it turned out, however, his considerable Irish charm eased things along for both of us.

One of the ways in which he resembled a Marine Gunnery Sergeant was his complete mastery of the tactic of surprise. He could quickly ask a question that would throw one completely off balance. Almost the first question he asked me was, "Do you believe that St. Brendan discovered America?" I had certainly never given the matter much thought, but I somehow guessed that Father George Brendan McCarthy had not only done so but had come to the conclusion that St. Brendan had arrived on the shores of the New World much before the Italian Columbus. Consequently, I responded, "If you say so, it may be so. I always respect the opinion of a pastor and you are the pastor here."

This response appeared to convince him that we might get along and he boldly decided to have me come to say a Mass each Sunday, not knowing how in that largely Irish parish I would be received, for I was not only married but had once been a minister in the Episcopal Church, which was the next thing to the Church of England.

None of us need have worried about how the people of St. Mary's would react. They received me with kindness and friendship from the very first. At once, I enjoyed my visits to St. Mary's, which is a beautiful example of excellent nineteenth century Gothic style, much as is Grace Church in Newark, where I had first known the best of Anglo-Catholic priestly ministry as it was exemplified by Charles Gomph.

Indeed, it looked so much like Grace Church that it brought out an unexpected problem for me and one which I had not anticipated. There came to the surface in my mind a very strange sense of having moved backwards in time. Suddenly things were, apart from my marriage, as they had been in 1941, except that now I was really a Catholic priest in the Catholic Church and not an outsider admiring it and looking at it from a distance. But I wanted the Church to be—and I wanted the priesthood to be—as I had imagined these things to be back in 1941.

Consequently, I closed my mind, wherever possible, to anything that suggested the contrary. There was, of course, no way of avoiding the pedestrian English of the vernacular Mass where once there had been Latin, but I wanted at least to use none but the Roman Canon. My first Sunday, and a few Sundays thereafter, I arrived for Mass wearing the long black cassock or soutane, something that had been common in 1941 but which is seldom seen in parish churches these days. I think I stopped wearing it only after someone asked me if I was a Jesuit. Any illusions I might have had about how things once were or how things were now in the parochial priestly ministry were generally dissipated quite quickly at St. Mary's, which was a lively parish of about fifteen hundred families served faithfully and well by George McCarthy and his assistant, Father Jack Unsworth.

But there was a good deal that required a lot of adjusting on my part. There were male and female Eucharistic ministers who were permitted to take the Blessed Sacrament out of the tabernacle at Communion time and to return it afterwards, while three priests knelt. There had been nothing like that in 1941, nor was there anything like that in the rather conservative parish I had attended most recently as a layman. I was likewise unused to Sunday Masses during which children were baptized and I found it distracting to have to endure Masses that included an instructional dialogue with First Communion classes, the little members of which later stood, or squirmed around the altar during the Canon.

I also had a great deal to learn about the special Irish ethos that permeated much of that place, whose pastor at any rate claimed St. Brendan as the man who had discovered America. There were, for example, three major feasts: Christmas, Easter, and St. Patrick's Day or, more exactly, the Sunday closest to it. That this Sunday was a Sunday in Lent made no

190 · *Where St. Brendan Discovered America*

difference, for it was kept with special festal splendor. The
Gospel was read in Irish Gaelic, a language that was not
understood by most of the parishoners; the flags of the Irish
counties adorned the sanctuary; and "Danny Boy" was the
final musical selection.

After some time, however, I found myself more or less
part of the scene at St. Mary's and increasingly aware of how
much I had to learn from its pastor, whom I came to regard
as a friend. Indeed Bishop Angell got to calling us "the odd
couple" and told the congregation at one of the special St.
Patrick's Masses that if Father McCarthy and I got on as well
as we did, there was still hope for peace in Northern Ireland.

Thus while I never was able to penetrate all the complex
Celtic depths of the ancient world of Kerry that had helped
form the character of George McCarthy, I at least began to
learn from him what it had meant to be one of the generation of men ordained, as he was, in 1956. Trained in an old-
fashioned Irish seminary to become a member of a dis-
tinctive clerical caste for which obedience to higher authority was a fundamental principle, he had lived through all the
changes that followed upon Vatican II in the United States,
where he had come to serve in what was for him a strange
and foreign land. And he had survived it all, although he
knew priests who had simply left.

He customarily described himself in the following way: "I
am not what is called a liberal, nor am I a conservative; I am
an open-minded man." And so he really was and had to be
to confront the job he had to do in his time and place in an
age of great transition in the Church in the United States.

That job, with a few variations, was like the job of hundreds of priests of his generation who had the task and responsibility of the care of great parishes, which probably had
their greatest days behind them. Managing and maintaining
old buildings, including a huge rectory occupied only by

himself and one assistant; working with a large, and expensive lay staff; acquiring knowledge of computer science; working with a variety of parish committees; and having to conduct necessarily long and often boring weekly staff meetings to plan everything well in advance—all these, and more, were simply the very stuff of daily life for George McCarthy, who could remember when pastors seemed like monarchs and were, as he put it, "on the pig's back."

Very quickly, I found all this so fascinating and challenging that I asked to be allowed to share in it somewhat more than once a week, and with the agreement of the Bishop, I was allowed to become a "part-time Assistant" as of the first of January, 1985. Specifically, I made hospital and nursing home visits, performed liturgical functions, and offered some courses in the Adult Education Program. I sometimes stayed overnight and had a bedroom, as well as a study in the rectory.

By that time George was aware that Mildred and I had no desire to move into the rectory, which both he and Jack Unsworth had both understandably earlier feared to be the case. In fact, they had even wondered if we wanted to bring our seven children with us, until it was known that they were all adults living their own lives.

But as much as George had adapted to post-Vatican II changes, he simply did not know how to deal with the question of what to do about Mildred's possible involvement in parish life. There was, after all, no precedent. Consequently, his initial reaction was that she should stay at a distance—a very "safe" distance across Narragansett Bay at our home in Kingston. That she might well have made a positive contribution because of her office experience, training in Montessori teaching, and knowledge of church-related subjects did not occur to him as a feasible idea, any more than it had occured to Bishop Gelineau. Thus although Mildred and I were seen together at one or two major parish social functions, the people of St. Mary's never had the opportunity to know her.

Subsequently, near the end of the four and a half years that I was associated with St. Mary's and ever since that time, both Mildred and I shared many friendly occasions with George McCarthy and we count him among our good friends. But what neither he nor we ever discovered was what things would have been like had Mildred and I actually lived, not in the rectory, but in the parish while I was, at least part of the time, a priest at St. Mary's.

Sometime after Easter in the spring of 1985, I had a scheduled month's vacation, which gave Mildred and myself the chance to return to Italy. We went first to Rome and I had the quite overwhelming experience of concelebrating a Latin Mass with one of our Dominican friends in the Clemente chapel of St. Peter's, not far from the burial place of the Apostle, which is below it. My friend from Gallipoli, together with his sister, had been informed of this event and quite astonished me by appearing with her in the congregation.

After Mass and on the way to lunch at Alfredo's, my friend's sister said to me, "Father, you have just performed a miracle because you got my brother to go to Mass, which is something he hasn't done in many many years." Recalling that the Mass had been in Latin and that we had worn Renaissance style cut-out chasubles not much seen these days, I replied, "I'll bet he doesn't think that anything has changed since the last time he was at Mass." I have to confess that in spite of all I had learned at St. Mary's, I took comfort in that thought.

Our stay in Rome included a public audience with the Holy Father at which we were close enough to him to receive his blessing. We also went to what must have been an unprecedented tea in the apartment of an official of the Sacred Congregation for the Doctrine of the Faith who lived in the exclusively clerical confines of the Albergo del Clero. He talked with us at length about the Pastoral Provision, about which he was much concerned, as it was part of his responsibility.

Later we had the splendid experience of driving to Rimini and to Ravenna, with its glowing mosaics placed there in the Byzantine time before the final collapse of the Roman empire in the West. And we were spiritually refreshed by the wonder of Assisi, which is still vibrant with the traces of the steps of St. Francis.

Having come to know Father George McCarthy, we decided to do something we had never done before. We went to Ireland and down to Kerry, where I asked a man in a pub what he thought of the idea that St. Brendan had sailed from there to discover America.

He replied, "Sure, there can be nothing to that story when you realize they say there were six Irishmen in a skin boat and they sailed in it for three months. I've no doubt in my mind that they'd all have killed each other long before they made it."

In the lovely old town of Dingle, we were escorted around by an Irish priest, Father John Shanahan, whom we had met during a summer visit he had made to Newport. In the parlor of a convent, he introduced us to the Superior and her assistant by saying, with a bit of a twinkle in his eye, "This is Father Thomson from America, and this is his wife, Mildred." The assistant disappeared and within minutes the room was filled with nuns who had come to see this great curiosity.

Upon our return home, never really having penetrated the wonder and mystery of Kerry, I worked through the summer on the parish census, and continued with my usual other duties until the fall of the following year. Then, with the permission of Bishop Gelineau, my duties at St. Mary's were much diminished and I undertook a project at Providence College which I had long wanted to try. I undertook to teach a group of talented liberal arts honors students as their sole instructor in the Western Civilization course during their Freshman and Sophomore years as an experiment and a means of evaluating the course's effects over its full sequence on a group of able students. They told me at the end that they thought the whole thing was a memorable experience. What they meant, I am not sure, but I know that I had a wonderful time.

Wonderful or not, it had worn me out, or so it seemed at the time. Having reached the age of almost seventy-two and feeling a bit weary from my not unexciting life, I had asked Bishop Gelineau to put me on the retired list, which was done, without cost to the Diocese, for I now had a pension from Providence College. My retirement became official in September 1988, just a little over five years after my ordination. Having made history as the first married Catholic priest in Rhode Island, I suppose I also made history as the one with the briefest pastoral ministry prior to retirement.

My friend George says that I am probably too restless ever to have made much of a parish priest but that I might be all right as a teacher. There may be some truth in what he says. There usually is, especially when it comes to talking about parish work in the Catholic Church today. As for being restless, this applies, in a way, to all of us, for as Augustine says, that will always be our lot until we rest in God, Who made us for Himself.

I have no idea of what the future of the Pastoral Provision will be or what place it may have, if any, in helping to resolve the many problems affecting clerical life in the United States and elsewhere. It may raise problems of its own, but if they can be worked out wisely their resolution might be useful elsewhere.

In any case, I am grateful for the grace of God and for the wife and family He gave me. I am more than grateful that I was permitted finally to be a priest of the Catholic Church, which I love. Whether or not I have served it, or my family, well, God alone can say. Meanwhile, I do rejoice that I am at home in the Household of Faith, whose sign towers over the centuries to affirm the positive meaning of life and the ever-lasting love of God. There is, as there has always been, an often contentious family in that Household. And I have been more than a little contentious myself. But at the center there is, as if stretched out in tension upon a cross, the sign of the family's affection and unity, the successor of Peter. In communion with him the Household I live in, together with my wife, I recognize as the Household of the Apostles, of Augustine, of Thomas More, and I say , even as Peter once said, "Lord, it is good for us to be here."